The Ultimate Jo

See what others are saying about this book!

"Robb's book is a must read for every job seeker. By closely following his advice and strategies, individuals looking to get a job or change jobs are guaranteed to have a leg up on the competition. I look forward to sharing his road map to employment with colleagues who have friends or family who are looking for jobs."

—Richard Wahlquist, president and CEO, the American Staffing Association, www.americanstaffing.net

"Robb Mulberger knows more about what it takes to land a job in today's ultracompetitive marketplace than just about anyone on the planet! This book is a must read for anyone looking to crack the code on interviewing and landing his or her dream job."

—David A. Rich, certified speaking professional and best-selling author of *How to Click with Everyone Every Time*, www.contagioustalk.com

"New college grads—this is must reading! The competition is fierce out there ... You need to read this book and follow its guidelines!"

—Marshall Brown, certified career and executive coach, Marshall Brown & Associates, www.mbrownassociates.com

"I have known Robb Mulberger for over thirty years, and he is and has been one of the most insightful people in the staffing industry. This book is filled with priceless gems. Don't skip a word of it, and you will discover tremendous personal and business value."

—Tim Connor, global sales, management, and leadership speaker and trainer and best-selling author of over eighty books, www.timconnor.com

"An excellent and thorough road map and handbook to get you through the career transition process. An excellent guide to get you focused like a laser on the employment process."

—Angelo P. Agrafiotis, president and founder, AAIM Life Coaching, http://www.aaimlifecoaching.com

The Ultimate Job Seeker's Guide

Robb Mulberger

First published by Dog Ear Publishing
4010 W. 86th Street, Ste H
Indianapolis, IN 46268
www.dogearpublishing.net

ISBN: 978-1-4575-1756-3

This book is printed on acid-free paper.

Printed in the United States of America

Preface

I have toyed with writing this book for years. Matching people and jobs has been my life's work. Over the years, I conducted hundreds if not thousands of training sessions, workshops and seminars, and gave numerous speeches regarding the process of matching people and jobs. Early on, I was on the firing line—as a recruiter finding candidates for organizations with a job to fill, matching people and jobs, coaching job seekers about their resume and interviewing. Later, I managed these processes and finally ended up owning and running a regional staffing services firm - NRI Staffing Resources of Washington, DC. Along the way, I served as a director and finally president of the industry's trade association, the American Staffing Association.

For as long as I can remember, I have dispensed advice about the job-seeking process to friends and family. When people have asked about having their resume professionally written, I have advised against it and said, "Send it to me... and I'll edit it for you". When people have considered engaging a career consultant – often for thousands of dollars, I have said "Buy me lunch and I will give you for free what they are gonna tell you." In particular, I coached them regarding "Uncovering the Hidden and Unpublished Job Market" – Chapter 9 of this book.

2008-9 saw a meltdown of the U.S. and world economies... what economists have ranked as the worst recession since the great depression. Recessions have always meant layoffs, and each successive recession since those of the1980s has been reflective of more jobs in the service sector and less in manufacturing...hence a recession means white-collar workers on the unemployment rolls. As noted, the recession that begun in 2008-9 is far deeper than others and has impacted people like no other recession; in some cases, entire families are out of work.

I knew that the knowledge I had accumulated over the years would be of value to many people... so I finally got around to committing to paper my experiences, thoughts and observations about the job-searching process. I hope they are of value to you.

Robb Mulberger

For all the people of the staffing services industry who make a difference in people's lives one job at a time.

Contents

CHAPTER 1

Successful Job Seeking—
An Overview and Some Absolutes
You Need to Know About the World of Work!

You may be looking for a job because you don't have one or because you don't like the one you have.

The same end result is desired, but different steps are to be taken, and different issues are to be addressed.

If you are at the right place at the right time, getting a job can almost be effortless. Most of the time, however, a person that gets a job offer has positioned him or herself to be *the* person to hire. He or she has successfully followed a process of executing step by step those activities that incrementally increase the odds of getting a job offer. That is what this book is all about—guiding job seekers through the dos and don'ts of the job-seeking process. Surprisingly, some of the most inept job seekers are those you would think would be good at it—those with extensive workforce experience. They have fallen victim to the "they don't know what they don't know, and what they do know is often wrong" mind-set.

We will examine the obvious topics—resumes and interviewing—in great detail. We will explore some advanced Internet search techniques, and we will examine how to unearth the "hidden and unpublished job market." We will explore what kind of research might be helpful, how networking comes into play, and how to decide which offer to accept once you are in that enviable position. We will cover the obvious resources—the Internet job boards and staffing services / headhunters. For those of you leaving the government (including the military), there are some different protocols to know and observe. There is a right way and a wrong way to resign from a job to take another, and we will cover

1

this in detail (somewhat of a "never burn your bridges" approach). And while it technically is not part of job seeking, we will discuss how to start your new job to maximize your success to get to your first anniversary there. Finally, we will discuss what to do to further leverage your career after you are established in your new job.

It is important to put into perspective some "absolutes" when it comes to the world of work and therefore the job-seeking process.

Two absolutes when it comes to people in general

When we examine why people do things (and don't do things), it is helpful to know about the two "radio stations" everyone listens to:

- WII-FM and WDTM-FM

- WII-FM = "What's In It For Me"

- WDTM-FM = "What Does This Mean For Me"

Nowhere is this truer than in the world of work, and without being cynical, we will take into account how these two dynamics impact why and how people do things. Just always keep in mind that people will usually do what is in their best interests more often than not—and that is fine until it conflicts with what the boss wants or organizational objectives!

Seven absolutes of the world of work and jobs

Let's next establish some absolutes in the world of work and jobs, and as you review them, keep in mind everyone's two favorite radio stations, and see how they come into play.

1. Every organization—and every manager—from the CEO to the newest supervisor wants these three things:

   - High output

   - Low cost

   - No problems

Therefore, to make the cut, you need to demonstrate that you have historically been a high-output person or offer that potential, and you are not a problem person.

Your salary cost must be within the range for the position and be a good value, considering your predicted capability to perform and achieve results. You must offer "job leverage" - the value of your output must exceed what you cost your employer! Those costs include salary, benefits, the space you occupy, and the equipment and resources you need to do your job. The "go to" [1] people in organizations always fit this model because, in addition to their assigned jobs, duties, and responsibilities, they can be counted on to fill in wherever needed, providing both answers and solutions—and do so without complaint or the expectation of anything in return other than knowing that they helped out.

High-output people arrive early, do their work on time and without errors, and do more than is expected or asked of their job descriptions. They also fit the low-cost mode—they don't abuse the lunch hour, breaks, or sick and vacation leave policy. They recognize the difference between "being sick" (staying at home) and not feeling totally up to snuff (coming to work). Nothing frosts a supervisor more than having a worker who seems to always miss a day every other week or so—and often on Mondays or Fridays—because of "not feeling well." High-output people don't feel that that they have to use every sick day and personal leave day "coming to them." They recognize that a day not at work costs their employers money (time IS money) and puts an additional burden on their coworkers.

If they have the ability to spend company money, they do so wisely. If they have an expense account, it is always reasonable.

Your references need to reflect that you are a team player and get along well with people—you are a "no problem" person and employee. Football great "T.O." Terrell Owens, despite his great football skills, was traded several times because he was a "problem" to his teammates, his coaches, and his owners.

And oftentimes, "problem people" haven't a clue! They are very self-focused, often view their world as "me versus the world," and are rarely

[1] "Go to" people are those that are of high value, are heavily recruited by other organizations, and are almost never let go in a layoff. Your objective is to be one of them in every job you have.

3

willing to concede any perceived perk or entitlement. Ever have a review less than stellar in that area? Do peers like and respect you? If not, why? Maybe you need to get to work on these skills.

What Does This Mean For Me: Focus your job-searching efforts where your experience and skills can generate "job leverage" and recognize the value of being viewed as a "high-output and no-problem" employee—and always be working toward that objective.

2.   The rules of supply and demand prevail.

The principle of supply and demand truly illustrates a major dynamic of the job market. If you are a research astronomer, you had best live near a planetarium or a large research university because there is not much of a demand elsewhere! If you are a brand-new college grad, be aware you are one of many; there is a big supply every spring. December college grads have an easier time finding jobs because there are fewer of them (supply) vying for the available jobs (demand).

This cycle repeats itself in many an industry—a housing boom means a high demand for mortgage loan processors. The initial low supply of them means big incomes as a result but only initially because people flock to become one, and pretty soon, the supply matches the demand, and mortgage companies can hire for less. Then there is a bust in the housing market and no need for as many mortgage loan processors, resulting in many who are then let go (no demand—large supply). If you made six figures plus because you rode the housing boom as a loan processor, guess what? Hope you saved some of it because until that demand comes back, you will be doing something else and probably making less.

When considering a career path, job search, or career change, factor in the supply-and-demand dynamic. There are many sources of data as to which jobs, industries, and careers are on the upward trend ... and which ones are headed south. Review these to give yourself a background canvas upon which to paint your career plans.

Keep in mind that the supply-and-demand dynamic is also location dependant. Larger markets and cities will have more sales and marketing opportunities than small towns and cities. Small towns and cities, on the other hand, are great places to find jobs in medicine and health care.

What Does This Mean For Me: Do your research about trends for various career paths of interest; you want to be in the mainstream, looking for a job in a field where there are jobs yet not a field that is swamped with candidates for those jobs.

3.   You are in competition for every job you seek.

And competition for jobs means comparison of capability and cost. If you are a whizbang staff accountant with a base salary of $XXX, you are in competition for that accounting manager slot with other staff accountants, some of which may have a base salary of $XX. If you can't justify the extra $X, guess what? You may well lose out to the $XX person. Willing to take a pay cut, you say? Hmmm ... would you hire someone who took a pay cut because he or she had to, hoping he or she will be there for the long term and won't be looking for a $XXX job soon after he or she came aboard? Me either. Human nature is that the newly hired pay-cut person will be looking before too long for a $XXX job.

Any employer that needs to fill a position has a certain supply of candidates from which to choose. The candidate that is offered the job is, in the opinion of the employer, the best combination of the following:

• Will do the best job

• Is the best fit personalitywise and will fit within the employer's culture without problems

• Is the most affordable

The balance between projected job performance and cost is an important consideration. (Remember the reference to "job leverage" above?) You will be evaluated in comparison to other candidates in light of your background and perceived ability to perform. Your salary requirements will also be compared to how much would be required to hire another available candidate to fill the position. You may well be the very best "qualified" candidate and still not get the offer if your salary requirements and/or salary history are higher than what the job is budgeted for—and your competition is capable of doing the job! The solution? Demonstrate that you are the "go to" person that—overall—has the greater "job leverage"!

This competitive issue includes some knockout factors to avoid:

• Keep the attitude positive—at all times.

Yes, you may be really annoyed (to put it mildly) at your former employer and former boss, but it will do you no good to voice that to prospective employers or staffing services. No one wants to hear about it, and it also paints you as a person who can't let go of the past and move on.

• Articulation and enunciation count.

If you sound like what you hear at the drive-through window of your favorite fast-food joint, you have a problem. You want to sound like the TV anchor on the evening news—clear voice and easy to understand. Ask those that know you well if you are articulate or a mumbler. Do you slur your words? Can you be clearly understood? Your first contact with a prospective employer will probably be on the phone, and if you can't be understood, you have a real problem being competitive. "Nice to meet you" isn't "Nice to meetcha!"

If English is not your first language and the jobs you are applying to require communicating in English, make it part of your plan to improve your written and verbal skills in English. Watch the TV news—strive to emulate the announcers. Read English newspapers. Stretch your vocabulary. Read aloud to someone with native English skills, and ask for critique. Your mission is to not let your communications skills stand in your way.

Have an enthusiastic voice—telephone and otherwise. Don't speak in a monotone or a flat voice. Answer your phone in a cheerful tone. Smile when you talk on the phone—the enthusiasm will come through!

And watch the phrases you use. Each generation has their own—but remember, you need to get past the screening of those you talk to. The best way to do that is to "mirror" them; subtly mirror their speaking styles. And notwithstanding your spiritual basis, skip the "Have a blessed day" in your correspondence, voice mail messages, and telephone sign off.

• Have a great resume

Without it, you are at a severe disadvantage. Carefully read chapter 7, "Your Resume: The Key to Your Next Job—Better Get It Right!"

- Dress in a contemporary manner.

Take a look at a fashion magazine or two. This extends to eyeglass style, necktie width, shoe style, hairstyle, and so on. The people who you first interact with at prospective employers may well be half your age. If your current or last job is/was for a significant period of time with one organization, you might not be very contemporary in attire. Don't look like you have stepped out of a twenty-year-old copy of *Time* magazine! Conservative business attire is always best, and you don't need to spend a bundle to be contemporary.

What Does This Mean For Me: Are you in fact competitive for the jobs you are interviewing for and seeking? If not, can you be? Or do you need to readjust your plan? If you realistically know you need to take a salary cut, you need to be convincing on that issue.

4. Every job is potentially at risk due to innovation, automation, and changes in the marketplace.

Remember our first absolute? Every organization and every supervisor every day is thinking of ways to increase output, lower costs, and minimize or eliminate problems.

- **Innovation -** Outsourcing is a perfect example. Outsourcing work to a firm that specializes in one narrow niche means no more internal work to be done regarding that function. For example, outsourcing payroll to a firm like ADP means no more payroll department jobs and no payroll department people issues (the people that do the work are the employees of the firm to which the work was outsourced).

- **Automation.** Get the same work done with fewer people through the use of computers, the Internet, and other automated systems.

- **Changes in the marketplace.** More and more people are reading fewer newspapers and magazines, getting their news and other information on the Internet. This has led to a significant reduction of newspaper and magazine advertising, which means far, far fewer ad salespeople as well as the jobs creating those ads. The drop in revenue from selling advertising has in turn been translated to staff cuts and to lower costs, hence fewer jobs on the writing and editorial staffs of newspapers and magazines. The bottom line is that changes in the marketplace have made print journalism not worker/career friendly! The same thing happened for the pager industry. Cell phones replaced many of the functions of pagers, hence there was no need for paging companies—hence market change eliminated much of an entire industry.

If there is a way for a staff of six to become a staff of four and still get it all done, it will/should happen.

Sometimes people that have been in the same jobs for five or ten years are surprised when their jobs are eliminated. There are no entitlements when it comes to jobs (except for maybe the US Supreme Court!). Just because there was a need for Ralph to do the same job for those ten years doesn't mean that it won't go away when efficiencies from automation or innovation eliminate the need for Ralph's job. Management is and needs to be relentless in finding ways to lower costs, and one of the most effective ways to do that is to lower the number of people doing a certain task.

Just like the paging industry, jobs that once existed in abundance that have been adversely impacted by innovation and marketplace changes include the following:

- **Secretaries and legal secretaries.** More and more supervisors, managers, and lawyers are expected to generate their own correspondence on their PCs. This is the same for other miscellaneous administrative tasks. The jobs are not as plentiful because the work performed is no longer there; it has been absorbed elsewhere.

- **Accounting clerks.** Automation and more sophisticated accounting software programs have resulted in far less work to be done in this area that needs human hands to do it.

- **Computer programmers.** Programmers were once the mainstay of the IT industry before the PC. The IT world consisted of large mainframes at computer service bureaus where computer programmers worked. You would take your task or project to the service bureau, where a programmer would write a program to do what you wanted to do—crunch numbers, do analysis, whatever. Then every week or month or whenever, you sent your data to the service bureau, and your work got done. Need a change in your report or analysis? A programmer needed to do it. Then along came the PC and packaged programs like Lotus, Excel, Access, and so on. Today, there are far fewer computer programmer jobs. Why? Because there is much, much less programming work to be done.

What Does This Mean For Me: What are the futures of the industries you are interested in interviewing with and exploring? Make sure it is not a dying or declining industry. For example, at the time of this writing, a career in Yellow Page sales or newspaper classified advertising sales is not advisable. Like almost any job at a newspaper or magazine, many have cut back significantly due to the impact of people getting their news and information online. On the other hand, careers in e-commerce and web design are projected to grow in the years ahead. As times goes on, always evaluate the WDTM-FM factors of *your* job. What is the future for the kind of work you do and the organization/industry that employs you?

5.   If you are a supervisor, your first loyalty is up, not down.

I once had a general manager of a branch office who, over time, more and more became an advocate for her staff—wanted more perks for them; wanted to accommodate their requests for more of this and more of that. And guess what? When she did, they wanted more. Yet productivity did not increase, and sales did not increase. There was no quid pro quo—nothing in return for all of her efforts (except they were very happy!). Her need to be liked surpassed her understanding of what her job was. She forgot that her first loyalty was to the mission of the organization—to achieve maximum profitability—and therefore operationally to her boss—me.

When I pointed this out to her, her first response—to be expected—was to justify her actions by stating that the way she kept her staff productive was through the things she did for them. To which I pointed out, "Fine, but make those things a payoff for the behavior and results you want, and never forget that your first job is to fulfill the organization's mission—a high level of productivity and profitability." I pointed out to her the reason she had a job is that I couldn't manage her office and do the other things I had to, and therefore, her job was to accomplish what I would do if I had her job rather than she.

Your job as a supervisor is to maximize the productivity of your people, holding them accountable for results. Take care of them, of course, and make sure they have the tools and environment to be successful, train them well, and listen to their concerns and issues—but not at the cost of productivity and profitability. This can be a particular challenge for a newly named supervisor, especially if your subordinates were your peers yesterday. Just remember that your first loyalty is up the organizational chart, not down.

What Does This Mean For Me: You simply can't succeed in the long run if you fail to recognize that your loyalty and focus has to be the organization's mission.

6. Job security resides in skill sets.

Are you or were you the "go to" person in your department? If not, why not? If not, then your skill sets are not the best in the department, and your job is potentially at risk. If you are / were, and you lose your job through no fault of your own, you will find a new job faster than someone who does not have the same level and degree of skill sets.

And there are two universes of skill sets:

- Hard skills—software skills, technical job knowledge, memory of past problems and issues and their resolution, application of basic business principles, strong writing skills, the ability to make strong oral presentations, and good negotiating skills

- Soft skills—problem-solving skills and the ability to find solutions, the application of common sense, a sense of curiosity that leads to figuring things out, a sense of logic and priority setting, good manners and etiquette, charm, and great people skills (see number seven below)

Your soft skills are reflective of your mind-set—your sense of self-esteem and self-value. Great soft skills are often characterized as "having your act together."

Your continuing "education" is your responsibility, no one else's. Some employers will offer access to training and education and maybe even pay for college, graduate school, or advancement courses. But keep in mind that it is *you* that is impacted the most by a lack of strong skill sets. Take advantage of the resources of your industry—trade association publications, published trends, technology issues. Access to almost all of it can be found online.

Good writing skills are a critical asset, and bad writing skills will hurt your career. The ability to convey a thought, concept, or course of action concisely, clearly, and without ambiguity is a necessity for many jobs and careers. You need to be able to "paint a mental picture" in words.

If in doubt as to whether or not you have "good manners," get a copy of *Emily Post's Etiquette* (now in its eighteenth edition!), and read it through. Good manners and etiquette will keep you from making many a faux pas and demonstrate that you are a person who can be counted on to act appropriately at all times. And this area includes what to say as well as what not to say. Successful people now and then have "bite marks on their tongues"—not uttering a word of a thought that crossed their mind until they do a quick reality check – is it appropriate? When in doubt, bite that tongue and keep quiet! Humor is indeed a two-edged sword, and what you think is cute or funny may be a breach of etiquette of the highest order! The world of politics is full of examples of some things better left unsaid!

If you aren't a reader of books that will help you grow, you are short-changing yourself. Sure, read the Western novels and whodunits you love, but don't overlook the stories of the great success and failures of others. They can be found in biographies, autobiographies, and stories of history. There is also no end to the timeless business books published in the past and new ones are hitting the shelves every day.

What Does This Mean For Me: I maintain that a study of the success and failures of others is the equivalent of an MBA in management, so if you travel the paths of George Washington, Robert E. Lee, and Dwight Eisenhower, to name just three, you can learn from their mistakes and emulate what made them successful, to say nothing of having a wealth of anecdotal information at your fingertips.

7. More people are fired, hired, promoted, or not promoted based upon interpersonal communications and conflict-resolution skills than any other single reason.

How are yours? Do you pass the "Tulsa Test"?[2] Do you naturally get along with people? Are you the person people want to sit next to at

---

[2] Tulsa Test: a total stranger would enjoy sitting next to you on a long-distance flight to Tulsa and, furthermore, would tell his or her friends about his or her delightful seat companion.

social or business occasions or the one no one wants to sit next to? We all know obnoxious people that are the last ones we want to sit next to or even talk with. Are you sometimes rude or brusque with people? Are you able to argue your cause without antagonizing people? Do you display lots of obvious **What's In It For Me?**

In fact, much of the key to this lies in eliminating from yourself those things that drive other people crazy in addition to being charismatic yourself.

There really is nothing more important in the world of jobs and employment than the ability to get along with people and inspire trust, confidence, and loyalty.

And this applies at all levels. One only needs to see the reason given for a Fortune 500 CEO's dismissal as "management style" to know that what this really means is that the CEO couldn't get along with the people he or she needed to work with.

So keep in mind that there is a difference between confidence and arrogance—and assertiveness versus aggressiveness—and that one of the objectives is to just be a likeable person.

Summary

- Always keep in mind why people do things and what motivates them to act in a certain manner—WII-FM and WDTM-FM.

- Remember the seven absolutes of the world of work and jobs:

  - Remember what organizations and managers want: high output, low cost, no problems.

  - Understand that the rules of supply and demand apply.

  - You are in competition for every job you seek—and you need to avoid the knockout factors.

  - Every job is at risk due to innovation, automation, and marketplace changes.

  - A supervisor's loyalty is up—not down—the organizational chart.

- Job security resides in skill sets.

- Hone and perfect those people and conflict resolution skills.

- If you keep these "absolutes" in mind as you go through the job-seeking process, it will keep things in perspective and help you understand the dynamics that govern how it all works! In fact, keep these absolutes in mind throughout your working life and whenever you wonder why people do things (or don't do things). Don't forget to examine their actions in light of **"What's In It For Me"** (WII-FM) and **"What Does This Mean For Me"** (WDTM-FM).

CHAPTER 2

Job-Seeking Strategy When You Are Unemployed— Or It's Time to Crank Up the Urgency Level!

Are you unemployed as a result of the current state of the economy in the post-2008/09 meltdown?

Well, the only good news is that you are in good company. It seemed that the news week after week and month after month was of massive layoffs. Mainstays of the US economy—General Motors, Lehman Brothers, Bank of America, Merrill Lynch, and so on—either went under, had to be bailed out by the feds, or barely squeaked by.

Stories abound of the difficulty of the unemployed to find jobs, especially newly minted college grads and older workers.

The objective of this chapter is to give you a concrete plan, a course of action, and some confidence builders. Each of the following chapters of this book has step-by-step actions you can take to put you in the best possible position to get the job offer you want or even just any job offer if you are in an "I'll take anything" mode. Let's all hope that the intensity of the current tough economy changes for the better soon, but anyone that is unemployed and finding it difficult to keep plugging away searching for employment will find this chapter helpful.

And if you are reading this well after the impact of that meltdown has passed, the steps to find a job when unemployed are as valid now as then.

Anyone that is unemployed involuntarily after a long period of time with one employer is going to have to work hard to keep things in perspective. They went from security and familiarity to uncertainly and abandonment—enough to unnerve the strongest of us, especially for older and/or more highly paid workers and those with a specific long-

14

term skill set whose jobs have just "gone away" (an auto worker let go because the plant closed; a senior auditor in a smaller city or town whose employer just went through a shutdown and liquidation; the finance and insurance manager at a long-established auto dealership that closed when the manufacturer pulled the plug on the dealership).

Worrying about your plight does absolutely no good. Commiserating with others might help but only in the short term. As "the Boss" Bruce Springsteen sings in "My Hometown," "Foreman says these jobs are goin', boys, and they ain't coming back." Well, in many cases, your job isn't coming back—at least as you knew it. Vent what you need to vent to some patient soul in your support system—spouse, close friend, whomever. It may take more than one venting to get over it, but if after a week, you are still at it, you are missing the point. It is what it is. Time to move on as best you can, but move on you must. Just as the warmth of spring follows the gray cold of winter, so shall there be better times for you.

As an entrepreneur responsible for the jobs of many, when challenging times have hit—and there have been plenty over the years—I have learned that during those times you really discover your inner strengths and how to focus.

During those times over the years, I have developed a mental and physical coping mechanism I refer to as "hunkering down." The process is one of clearing your mind from all the extraneous stuff—cancel meetings, trips, and the like that are distractions and just soak up your time. Cut your "just filling time" reading load—catalogs and magazines. You are buying time, time to do just two things. Be able to think, and then do the really big things that matter. I think of Abraham Lincoln's response to some critic complaining that Lincoln was not giving attention to some bureaucratic issue of the day during the Civil War. Abe said, "If I don't save the Union, it won't matter ... and if I do save the Union, it will be forgotten." Clearing your mental calendar to think and then act will have the significant side impact of keeping your spirits up and your attitude strong and positive.

I am sure others have a variation of this process, but the point is that unless you have your mental game together, you are not going to be very effective resolving the issue. The tactics are not complicated—take care of the more important things first, and do something concrete and positive every day. Day by day, do those things that will incrementally achieve your objective(s). Don't worry about or even think about those things you can't change or influence. It does no good to toss and turn during the night and not get a decent night's sleep. The critical aspect of this coping mechanism is to regularly step away from your day-to-day "where am I so far" report card and look at the situation from a thousand feet up. Take stock of your progress, and from up there, you can see on the horizon—somewhat fuzzily—better times, and the wind is drifting them your way. The right actions always bring results; in really tough times, it just takes longer. Stick to the basics.

Here are two more basic observations about being unemployed, especially if you were one of the victims of the 2008/09 US economic meltdown and the resulting US economy:

1. Time is not on your side. It will take longer than usual to find your next job, so get on with it—right away and every day. More below on this.

2. We all—but especially those that were pretty far up the economic and employment "food chain"—need to keep in mind that people that used to be really important need to remember that they are no longer really important when they are looking for jobs. The world doesn't owe you a job, so don't come across to the contrary. See absolute number seven in chapter 1.

As explained in chapter 1, you are going to be in competition for every job you apply for and interview for. Early on, you want to eliminate the obvious knockout factors. Read about them in chapter 1. If you were employed for a significant period of time with one organization before you became unemployed, chances are you may not be "up to speed" with those you will be competing with for your next job. Follow the advice in this book to be more competitive in your job search.

When searching for a job while unemployed, there are three important things to do:

1. Keep your spirits and attitude up.

2. Watch your financial resources carefully.

3. Treat looking for a job as a full-time job.

1. Keep your spirits and attitude up.

This is far easier to say than do, but it is critical to shortening the time you are unemployed. Don't let the situation of being unemployed and facing what appears to be an impossible task put you in a funk.

Keep in mind that when unemployment is 6% or 7% or 8%, that means that 94% or 93% or 92% of the workforce is employed. Be assured, you will get a job. The issue is how soon. So banish the fear that you will be unemployed forever. Look at it this way: every day you are unemployed is one day you are closer to getting your next job.

But back to the issue of keeping your spirits up and your attitude positive as you go through your job search process and efforts. Spending some time—every day if possible—doing positive things will reinforce a positive mind-set. Only you can control and influence your mind-set, and you need to do things to keep it positive. Do daily exercise. Work out and stay healthy. A brisk walk is a great option. When you exercise, you are not only staying fit, you are generating endorphins that in turn give you a natural "high". And if you are overweight and out of shape because you "never had time to exercise," well, now you do! Get on with it!

In addition to staying physically fit and healthy, work a few hours one afternoon or on a Saturday in some sort of volunteer activity. Work at a Habitat for Humanity restock center, volunteer at a local hospital or hospice, be a resource of sorts at a local school. There are many opportunities for volunteerism. The important thing is that you will be accomplishing something positive—being of value to others—and that will help to implant a can-do mind-set.

Read one of the many great self-help books that are available. My author-speaker-trainer friends Tim Connor (www.timconnor.com) and David Rich (www.contagioustalk.com) have some great ones that you will find motivating and uplifting.

Whatever method you choose, make it part of your daily and weekly schedule; your attitude and self-worth will come through during interviews and other job-seeking activities, and you must project yourself as being positive! And do keep in mind that every person you talk to, interact with, and work with should be the subject of your efforts as noted in chapter 9, "Job-Seeking Strategy - Uncovering the Hidden and Unpublished Job Market."

Don't take it personally

Searching for a job while unemployed is tough—and even more so if your financial resources are not strong enough to prevent cold sweats and panic. You may be unemployed because you are a new college grad and still seeking your first "real" job. Your circumstances may be due to a merger where your job was eliminated, your organization relocated and you chose not to move, a general layoff due to economic and market conditions, or you may have been terminated for cause. Keep in mind the line from the movie *The Godfather*, "It isn't personal … just business." With the exception of a termination for cause, you are simply a victim of being in the wrong place at the right time. However, do recognize that you were laid off and others weren't. "Go to" people are rarely laid off, so think back as to what you might have done to have not been one of the ones let go. Think back as to who the "go to" people were and what you could have done to be one of them. This self-analysis is important so that you don't make the same mistakes twice; in your next job, a pressing objective is to indeed be one of the "go to" people.

If you were terminated for cause, you need to really figure out where things went wrong and work to resolve that issue or performance-related shortfall because you will be called upon to explain it during interviews.

Do some soul-searching

Before jumping into the job-seeking process, take a day or so to do some soul-searching. What are you good at? Where are your strengths? And likewise, what are the areas that have proven to either not be strengths or that you don't enjoy? Not every aspect of every job needs to be fun, but every job needs some fun aspects to it. Use this time to really examine what is important to you so that your search takes you in that direction. Many people in similar situations have used the challenge of finding a new job while unemployed as a chance to reinvent themselves. Lawyers become teachers, retail salespeople become HR recruiters, and so on.

Sound out those who know you well—family, friends, a spiritual mentor. Engage them in a conversation of why they like what they do and why they ended up in their vocations. If you have friends/contacts in academia, talk to them about the trends they see in their academic areas. And as you did with those you interacted with while keeping your spirits up, chapter 9 applies to these people whose counsel you seek as well.

2.   Watch your financial resources carefully.

Unemployment compensation

Immediately upon being unemployed, file for unemployment compensation. There is no negative attached to doing so. Society has put it in place to assist people who need help. It will give you a bit of a financial cushion as your pursue your job search. Your local unemployment office can be found in the phone book or via an Internet search.

Other financial issues

If you have severance, spend it carefully. Know your former employer's benefit structure to know what you are entitled to. Take stock of unused sick leave (usually not paid) and unused vacation pay (you are almost always entitled to it). Strongly consider going on COBRA coverage for health care insurance; to not have health insurance is taking a big risk.

Unless you have a sizeable nest egg, dramatically slash all discretionary expenses. You don't know how long you will be unemployed, and you don't want your back against the wall moneywise. Dump the double-whatever latte, and don't renew magazine subscriptions or those myriad of small memberships we seem to accumulate. Cancel the premium cable. Cut way back on going out to anything. Your friends will understand!

3. Treat looking for a job <u>as a full-time job</u>.

The mind-set you want when searching for a job while unemployed is to treat it as a full-time job. Get up at an (early!) fixed time every day, and begin to execute the plan you created the day before.

A good schedule to follow is the following:

7:30 a.m.–8:30 a.m.	Check e-mail, respond – print hard copies, and file.
	Check your calendar to see what appointments and interviews you have scheduled.
	Review the list of calls you are going to make later this morning.
8:30 a.m.–noon	Make telephone calls and follow up, respond to online and classified ads, send resumes and cover letters to targeted organizations.
Noon–1:00 p.m.	Lunch. Take a brisk walk. Read industry trade journals, business publications, such as *Business Week*, the *Wall Street Journal*, and so on. You need to stay in contact with what is going on in the world of work.
1:00 p.m.–4:00 p.m.	Continue with the morning's plan of making and returning telephone calls and e-mails, responding to ads, and so on.
	Spend some time doing something that makes you feel good about yourself—community service, participating on webinars of interest and value, working out at a gym or the Y, and so on. You need this to keep your spirits up and strong as noted above.
4:00 p.m.–5:00 p.m.	Plan the next day – write it down – mental lists are not sufficient! —call lists, calendar items (appointments and interviews).
	Take care of any details that didn't get done during the day.

Of course, interview whenever the opportunity presents itself!

Don't let distractions get in the way of keeping a schedule. If you find your mind wandering, get a cup of coffee or take a short walk. It can be hard to stay focused when you are working on your own at home, but keep at it. And don't even think of turning on the TV!

Evening	Relax, have a nice dinner, read an interesting book, go to bed at your normal bedtime. This is not the time to stay up to watch late-night TV. You want to wake up on time the next day feeling rested and refreshed to have a go at it again.

Take a temp job while you look?

What are the advantages of taking a temp job while you look? It will put a weekly paycheck in your pocket, and you will be "interviewing" while you work—you will be demonstrating to the organization for whom you are temping what your capabilities are and how you are performing for them. Press your staffing service to put you on assignments that have a chance of turning into a full-time job via the temp-to-hire route.

The downside is that you no longer can treat looking for a job as a full-time job. You owe it to your staffing/temp firm employer and the organization to which you have been assigned to give full-time and best efforts to the work to be done.

So the decision boils down to economics. If you can sustain yourself for ninety days, make your job for fifty to sixty of those days to be a full-time job seeker. If after sixty days you aren't seeing some activity that looks like it will lead to one or more job offers, reevaluate. How are your resources? Can you go another thirty, sixty, or ninety days? If so, consider again working full time to find a job. Just leave yourself a thirty-day cushion to find a temp job so you aren't totally high and dry.

Regardless, however, register immediately with one or more select staffing services / headhunting firms; you want to be in their databases as soon as possible so as to not miss out on an opportunity.

When you register with staffing services / headhunting firms, be sure to choose those that also provide temporary help services. Be upfront with your recruiter about what your plan is. Tell your recruiter that you could accept some short-term (a week or less) assignments, but for the short term, you want to focus on finding a permanent job and want the recruiter to do the same. Tell the recruiter you will keep him or her informed of your efforts. Make yourself totally available to the recruiter to go on interviews for positions he or she has unearthed for you that are of interest. See chapter 6 for further information about working with a staffing services / temporary help service.

Should you consider relocating?

Here is where family considerations come into play. A spouse's job, parents nearby that count on you for assistance, and a special school for a child with special needs are all reasons why relocation is often not a viable option. It has been done, of course. But that doesn't mean that it isn't a real challenge.

On the other hand, if none of those barriers are present, consider it if it seems to make sense careerwise. Research all the options—growth trends, industry and job trends in the targeted areas, climate, and so on. It may be a chance to live in that part of the country (or world) where you always wanted to be.

Don't overlook a minirelocation. I live in Alexandria, Virginia—just across the Potomac River from Washington DC. A job in Leesburg, Virginia (forty-five miles away), is out of the question due to the commute, but not if I lived in Reston, Virginia. A twenty-mile relocation makes the job in Leesburg viable. This same concept applies to most major metropolitan areas.

Summary

If you are one of the unfortunate people that lost their jobs in the economy that emerged from the economic meltdown of 2008/09, you have some unique challenges.

Recognize that "it is what it is," and get on with the tactics in this book.

Recognize what you need to do to be competitive in the job market.

When searching for a job while unemployed, there are three important things to do:

1. Keep your spirits and attitude up.

- Don't take being unemployed personally—regardless of why.

- Do some soul-searching—determine your strengths and soft areas.

2. Watch your financial resources carefully.

   - File for unemployment compensation—there is nothing negative about that.

   - Conserve cash.

   - Consider COBRA for benefits; to not have health care insurance is taking a big risk.

3. Treat looking for a job as a full-time job.

   - Consider temping while looking for a full-time job.

   - Consider relocation.

CHAPTER 3

The Steps to Your Next Job—And Avoiding Any Missteps

Unless you get very lucky or your wonderful uncle Ralph has a place for you in the family business, you are going to find your next job through a series of repetitive actions—submitting resumes, interviewing, and so on.

Anytime you are going to do anything multiple times, it makes great sense to figure out the best series of processes to achieve your objective and then make that the cookie-cutter approach. "Cookbook" the process, if you will.

Below are the steps you will travel to obtain that next job. Skip any of them at your own risk. We will discuss several of them here; others are stand-alone chapters in this book.

1. Define what it is you want and don't want. What are your core values, and how do they impact your work?

2. Get organized.

3. Basic research is essential.

4. Prepare your resumes and cover letters.

5. Prepare to interview.

6. Should you post your resume on an Internet job board? Which ones? How transparent/confidential are these postings?

7. Know how to use the Internet and how to do advanced Internet searches.

8.   Should you use a temporary help service / staffing service / head-hunter? How do headhunters operate?

9.   Reach out, make those calls, and establish those contacts.

10. Respond to inquiries, and schedule interviews.

11. Refine your resume and interview responses.

12. Evaluate job offers; negotiate salary and benefits.

13. Accept and turn down offers.

14. Resign from your current job if employed.

15. Start your new job.

16. Time for some career planning—what next?

1.   Define what it is you want and don't want. What are your core values, and how do they impact your world of work?

Not everyone wants to be rich, a CEO, or even a manager of people. Think through where your successes (and failures) have been. Recall your past performance reviews. Think of the good and bad bosses you have had in the past and what you learned from them about the world we live in and the world of work. How important is family time to your everyday life? If you want to attend every little league game, every field hockey game, and every school play, a job with fifty or sixty hours of work a week—or one with heavy travel—is incompatible with your family objectives.

On the other hand, it takes sacrifice and getting priorities in order to succeed in the world of work. The reality is you *will* miss a few of those games, but your choice of a career path will often determine how many.

Include in this self-examination such issues as big company versus small, what the future holds for the various industries and jobs you are exploring, how much of a commute you are willing to make, and how important money is to you versus "quality of life" issues.

If you don't do well with continuous multitasking, make sure that is part of this self-analysis. If you don't do well without close direction and continual feedback, don't pursue a career with lots of independent work.

Nowhere is "Know thine own self" more important than when making career and job decisions.

2. Get organized.

You are going to talk to lots of people, get lots of e-mail and regular mail, generate lots of correspondence, and have a number of interview answers and questions. Therefore, you need to be totally organized. To not do so is to conduct your job search in a half-baked manner. See chapter 4, "Job-Seeking Strategy 101—Logistics and Getting Organized."

3. Basic research is essential.

You need to research the industries you are considering, the kind of jobs you are exploring, the organizations you are looking at, and finally, the interviewer(s) you will be meeting with. Never has this been easier; in the pre-Internet and pre-Google days, it meant trips to libraries and many phone calls.

In many cases, this research is significantly simplified by what you have done in the past; most people stick with their basic expertise—accounting/finance, sales/marketing, and so on. This narrows the range of research options, but you still need to know, to the extent of information available, what the future holds for your next employer as well as a little of the background of the interviewers you will face. More and more, the people you will be interviewing with have LinkedIn profiles. You need to read them. See chapter 5, "Basic and Advanced Internet Search Techniques."

Think carefully about some basic criteria:

• What industries are you interested in and seem capable of weathering, whatever the future may hold for them? What industries and jobs seem to be trending upward in growth, popularity, and stability?

• Consider location based upon your commute, including public transportation and locations where you would be willing to move (a local move) or relocate (move to a different city or state).

As a result of this thinking and study, prepare a target list of twenty to twenty-five companies, nonprofits, government agencies, and other employers. This is your initial target list (you may add others as these are explored and discarded as possibilities). In addition to whatever job opportunities come your way, you want to find a way to get your credentials in front of a decision maker at each organization on your target list. You will do this by utilizing your network to see who knows who and by using the techniques described in chapter 9, "Job-Seeking Strategy—Uncovering the Hidden and Unpublished Job Market."

You can't remember it all, so print all of the pertinent information you have gathered doing this research, or create an MS Word file with your notes. Get organized as noted in number two above. Note the Internet bookmarks so you can return to your sources if needed (this is discussed in more detail in chapter 5, "Basic and Advanced Internet Search Techniques").

4. Prepare your resumes and cover letters.

Do not proceed further until you have done this. The resume and cover letters are the basic tools you need to proceed. See chapter 7, "Your Resume: The Key to Your Next Job—Better Get It Right!"

5. Prepare to interview.

This is where the time invested to prepare will pay off big time. You should never, never answer a question for the first time in a live interview. You should anticipate *every* question you will be asked and then prepare a *written* answer which you will rehearse until you know it cold. See chapter 8, "Interviewing—The Bridge Between You and Your Next Job."

6. Should you post your resume on an Internet job board? Which ones? How transparent/confidential are these postings?

The answer is yes, but recognize the risk. Your current boss (or a coworker) may well find out that you have done so, and that is probably not good unless you have discussed with him or her what your plans are for moving on.

Notwithstanding this risk, however, the job boards give your resume far greater exposure than you could ever achieve on your own. Some of them permit you to post it without revealing your name; others don't.

Check them all out. Ask friends and acquaintances which job boards they have used and what their experiences were before you post. Check out any blogs or message boards with information about them.

There are many, many job boards—some national and general in scope, and others are regional and/or industry specific. The well-known national and general ones at the time of this writing are Monster, CareerBuilder and Yahoo! HotJobs. The region- or industry- specific ones are too numerous to list, so just do an Internet search for them (e.g., "accounting Internet job board"). See chapter 5, "Basic and Advanced Internet Search Techniques."

7.   Know how to use the Internet and how to do Internet searches.

No doubt you have done Internet searches, but in your job search, you need to hone the manner in which you search to cut down on how much time you will invest to get the information you seek. Do an Internet search on "how to search the Internet," and read on. See chapter 5, "Basic and Advanced Internet Search Techniques."

8.   Should you use a temporary help service / staffing service / head-hunter? How do headhunters operate?

Yes, by all means, but be selective. A staffing service's role is to represent you to prospective employers, anonymously at first. As in the case of Internet job boards, they give you wide exposure while protecting your identity until there is interest on the part of a prospective employer. They also can negotiate on your behalf far more effectively than you can on your own. And be sure to include those that are temporary staffing services; they can put you to work as a temp, and in many cases, working as a temp is a viable step to a permanent-career job. See chapter 6, "How to Best Use a Staffing Service Company / Headhunter."

9.   Reach out, make and calls, and establish those contacts.

Fire up the job-seeking process! Start responding to both print classified ads and online ads and job postings on the job boards. Depending on what kind of a job you seek, don't overlook the breadth of job postings from Craigslist to the *Wall Street Journal* to your local government unemployment office.

Pursue the "hidden and unpublished job market"—see chapter 9.

If you are unemployed, treat job seeking as a full-time job. As noted in chapter 2, get up early, and execute the plan you created at the end of the previous day.

10.   Respond to inquiries and schedule interviews.

Let no time elapse in responding to e-mails, telephone calls, voice mails, and regular mail. Send nothing without proofing carefully. Write succinctly and to the point. With almost every response, send another copy of your resume (the one you submitted before! Which one is that, you say? Hmmmm … record keeping pays off, right?). Read chapter 4, "Job-Seeking Strategy 101—Logistics and Getting Organized."

11.   Refine your resume and interview responses.

As you interview and respond to questions, refine your written answers and perhaps even your resume. As you hear new or different questions, add them to your repertoire, and draft appropriate answers to them. Of course, you will be 99% prepared, but every now and then, you will be tossed a question you didn't anticipate. Answer the unique or oddball question as best as you can, add it to your notes later and script the perfect response. You may be asked it again!

12.   Evaluate job offers; negotiate salary and benefits.

Yes, sooner or later, you will get called back for second-level and third-level interviews (follow-up interviews with the same organization) that will lead to a job offer. You will want to time those offers as best you can, evaluate them carefully, and either accept or turn them down. If there has been good and open dialogue during the interview process, there will be surprisingly little to negotiate. If you are using a staffing service to find your next job, they will do the negotiating for you, usually far more effectively than you can do yourself.

13.   Accept and turn down offers.

When the time comes to accept an offer, – be gracious about it. "I am very excited about the future with XYZ Corp and can't wait to hit the ground running. Thank you for the offer. Let me confirm the details." And then indeed confirm all of the details: start date and location, immediate supervisor, and compensation and benefits details. Ask for a confirmation letter that details the specifics. If none is forthcoming, you confirm them in written form to the person who extended the offer.

When the time comes to turn down an offer, be even more gracious. "Thank you very much for the job offer. I am sure it is a great opportunity, but I don't feel that it is right for me. I really enjoyed our conversations, and I would like to stay in touch." Be prepared to tell why it wasn't a good fit, if asked.

Follow up by saying the same thing in writing—equally graciously—which will end up in your file, which is where your want it to be in the event that you are back interviewing with that same organization down the road. See chapter 12, "Congratulations! You Have an Offer! Now What? Evaluating Offers; Negotiating Salary and Benefits."

14.   Resign from your current job if employed.

This where the old adages "Burn no bridges" and "You never know who might be your boss—again" come into play. This is a time to be gracious and do nothing more than say good-bye. See chapter 12, "Parting Is Such Sweet Sorrow—Resigning ."

15.   Showtime—day one at your new job.

The day has arrived: first day at your new job! Exciting times!

Come prepared for an hour of more of paperwork, and bring along your documentation to legally work in the United States, insurance beneficiary information, and so on.

See chapter 13, "Showtime—Day One at Your New Job!"

16.   Time for some career planning—what next?

Now that you are employed, start to do some career planning. Many people spend more time planning vacations than they do their careers and career tracks. Don't be one of them; now is the time to begin some long-term career planning. See chapter 14—"Now What – Planning Your Career"

Summary

- Follow all the steps. Do your preparation, and you will maximize your success!

- They are all important to success, so take no shortcuts!

CHAPTER 4

Job-Seeking Strategy 101—
Logistics and Getting Organized

There are certain logistical tasks and procedures you need to put in place for the sake of efficiency and to eliminate some of the common roadblocks to a successful job search.

What kind of roadblocks are we talking about?

1. Not documenting action taken

    (Telephone ringing)

    You: "Hello, Bill the job seeker here."

    Caller: "Hello, Bill. Frank Harris of Biotech here, following up on the resume you sent us."

    You: (Feeling of panic. Which job were you responding to at Biotech??)

You need to be *totally* organized to be prepared to take these calls, and that calls for excellent documentation.

Solution: Create an Excel spreadsheet

- First column—name of potential employer

- Second column—person to whom you sent the resume (if you know it)

- Third column—job title you are applying for (unless you mailed a resume and cover letter without applying for a specific job)

- Fourth column—organization's telephone number

Then sort alphabetically all columns by the first column and print. Update with every new entry. Callers or contacts will almost always identify the organization from which they are calling. If they don't, just ask, "Can you tell me which company you are calling from?" You will never be stumped again as to who is calling about what job. This database will also help to decipher those cryptic voice mail messages. You usually can catch enough of the message to figure out who called regarding what!

You can easily add comments as background inserts. Put the cursor on any cell, and do a right click, which will bring up a drop-down menu. Click on "Insert Comment." Up pops a box in which you can type your comments, add information, and so on that would otherwise make your spreadsheet cumbersome. When you leave that cell/comment, what remains is a little red mark in the upper right-hand corner of the cell telling you there is a comment there. Simply positioning the cursor over the cell brings up the comment. A right click brings up a drop-down menu with "Edit Comment," which allows you to add to the comment or edit it.

2. Have an e-mail account that is web based, and have a grown-up e-mail address.

You want a web-based e-mail so you can check it from any Internet connection (and your PDA, a.k.a. smartphone, if you have one), not one you can only check at your home computer. There are many available (Hotmail, Yahoo! Mail, etc.), but as of this writing, Gmail from Google (www.gmail.com) is strongly recommended. It has a feature whereby the back-and-forth e-mails are linked to form a "thread"; all back-and-forth exchanges can be seen together in order, and it utilizes Google's search technology to find e-mails. Now that you have chosen which web-based e-mail program to use, you need to create an e-mail address.

So what if you were the star twirler on the cheerleading squad in college? An e-mail address of twirlerhottie@whatever.com just doesn't send the message you wish to communicate. If you don't want to use your full name in an e-mail address (and many don't), at least use an address that lets people know it is you. Include your first name, for example. I have a slew of friends with e-mail addresses like fishing-pal@whatever.com that defy me to recall who they belong to!

3. Avoid e-mail faux pas (or, you really should know better)!

E-mail is a critical part of the job-seeking process. You would think that as adults, we would all be aware of the potential pitfalls of e-mail, but they bear reviewing. There are many, but we will limit this section to e-mails in a job-seeking context.

- Watch that "Reply All" option! Be sure you know to whom the original e-mail was sent and copied and if you need to respond to *all* of them. If it is truly pertinent to the topic *and* it is important that all of the original recipients get that info, go ahead and click "Reply All." If it is not pertinent to all but rather a clarification that only impacts the originator, then just click "Reply."

- *Never* send an e-mail when angry, frustrated, or annoyed. Smart people have "bite marks on their tongues" and don't respond immediately to every slight, insult, or sarcastic remark sent their way. Draft your thoughts while they are fresh on your mind in your word processing program, and save it for review in a day or so. Sometimes by the time you review it, the need to respond may have passed. You certainly will edit it to be more matter-of-fact and neutral in tone than it was in its original form. You may edit the list to whom you send it. Remember, things "said" in anger usually represent you arguing for yourself rather than for the issue(s). Abraham Lincoln wrote many a letter that was never sent. He'd draft it, set it aside, later note on it "never sent," and file it away. You would be well advised to follow Abe's example! You are going to get rejection e-mails; the *only* way to respond is graciously.

- Watch your language! Never, never, ever use language in an e-mail that you aren't prepared to justify to your dear, sweet mom! You will never get in trouble in this regard if you follow the "*Washington Post* and Mama Rule." Never write anything you aren't prepared to see on the front page of the *Washington Post* (or your local newspaper), above the fold, and delivered to your mom's front door. Enough said!

- E-mail or a telephone call? When in doubt, make the call. E-mail is fine; e-mail tag is not. You can get more done in a five-minute telephone call than a dozen back-and-forth e-mails, and you can communicate tone and tenor much more effectively. And never use e-mail as an excuse to duck a tough conversation. That is just tacky!

- New topic? Then change the subject; otherwise you run the risk of the recipient assuming he or she knows the content and not reading it as soon as you intended. Make sure the subject is specific and to the point. Remember, people may be searching within their e-mails for a specific one, and the subject line needs to reflect the content.

- Brevity is appreciated, especially for folks reading e-mails on PDAs. If you need to say it, do so, but if it is more than a page or two, warn people in the subject line ("subject—LONG").

- Make sure the file names of attachments represent the content. The file name tells the recipients that it is legitimate (attachments are a huge carrier of computer viruses) and lets recipients know if they need to open it now if on their PDAs or if it can wait until they get to their desktops. If the attachment is a resume, be sure the file name identifies it as such—"HJackson_resume.docx".

- Use address autofill with caution. If you type R-o-b-e, Robert Harris comes up before Robert Thompson from your address book. Hit Enter too soon and the wrong Robert gets your e-mail.

- cos … gr8 … 2g2bt … gd4u. Yikes! Watch the text talk! It is great for your kids to use and maybe for you to text message your kids—or even your bridge club—but not for business e-mail. Use real grown-up words, please! BTW … oops … by the way, there is a great list of those abbreviations at http://www.txtdrop.com/abbreviations.php. (cos = because; gr8 = great; 2g2bt = too good to be true; gd4u = good for you.)

- Profff red and spale chek. Yes, be sure your grammar, sentence structure, choice of words, and examples and spelling reflect upon you as you would wish. Just because it is e-mail and not printed mail doesn't relieve you from writing as your long-ago English teacher taught you. Remember that spell-check thinks "red" is fine when you meant "read." You still need to proofread!

Okay, happy faux pas–free e-mailing!

4.   Have a telephone number that a kid won't answer.

Also ensure that it doesn't have some artsy prerecorded salutation. A good cell with the best service available will do fine. As of this writing, Verizon gets the best grades nationally, but check to see which carrier might be better in your area. Put your salutation on it. "This is Jim Jackson. Please leave your name, number, and a brief message, and I will get back to you as soon as possible."

Most importantly, never turn it off. Why? Because then any missed calls will indicate the number that called. The combination of how people rapidly leave their callback numbers, along with the sometimes shaky clarity still found with cell phones, can mean a message with a callback number you can't fully hear. Your "Missed Calls" log will have the number. Just put it on silent at night, during interviews, and so on.

Okay, so much for the potential roadblocks. What are the other logistical issues you need to take care of?

1.   Organize your computer.

Otherwise, you will find yourself searching for letters you have sent, which resume or cover letter you sent to whom, and so on. Set up a directory (often abbreviated as <dir>) called "Job Search." Within that <dir>, set up subdirectories for the following:

- **Resume templates.** These are all of the different resumes you have created and sent. Use the file name to distinguish them. At the same time, you don't want the file name to reflect that you do have different resumes so don't have file names like "HJackson_resume1.docx" and "HJackson_resume2.docx". Rather, label them as "HJackson_resume.docx", H.Jackson_resume.docx", "H_Jackson resume.docx", and so on. Print each version and pencil on it its file name for reference. If you are replying to ads for both controller and accounting manager (for which you will have different resumes—see chapter 7, "Resumes), you can incorporate that into the file name— for example, "HJackson resume controller.docx".

- **Cover letter templates.** Observe the same considerations as above. Create a <dir> for your different cover letters.

- **Organizations contacted.** Create a <dir> for each organization to whom you are submitting resumes and correspondence. Here save/file notes, PDF files of their website pages that you wish to be able to reference, PDF files of maps to find the interview location, copies of any e-mails you sent them and they sent you, and so on. In other words, keep a complete computer file for each organization you are corresponding with.

- **References.** Maintain your list of references and reference letters or documents if you have any (see chapter 7, "Resumes).

- **Interview answers and questions.** Keep your scripted answers to all of the questions you may be asked and the questions you will ask (see chapter 8, "Interviewing").

And do we need to remind you to back up this information to a hard drive, a CD, or an online backup service—daily? I didn't think so.

2.   Set up a manila file folder for each organization you will be contacting.

Put a hard copy of the information in it that you may be called upon to refer to (copies of resumes and cover letters submitted, etc.). Keep copies of everything, on paper and electronically; this file folder is for the items you might need to access without having to fire up your computer or those you want to take with you on an interview.

3.   Have a good, quiet place to work.

This might not be easy in a home environment, so get creative. Most importantly, you need to be able to have a telephone conversation without interruption—no dogs barking, no TV in the background.

4.   Have the supplies you need.

Ensure that you have printed resumes, blank paper for more resumes and cover sheets. Printer cartridges. Stapler. Envelopes, stamps—all of the standard office supplies you may need.

5.   Looks count—get a nice portfolio, pen, and personal "business" cards.

When you go on interviews, you will be taking some material with you—copies of your resume, information about the organization you are interviewing with, maybe directions about how to get there. You will need a nice portfolio to carry those things in; it doesn't have to be expensive, but it needs to look professional (has no advertising on it). Get one with a built-in memo pad that zips up to keep everything in place and prevent things from spilling out.

Have a nice pen—one with no advertising on it. Again, it doesn't have to be an expensive one.

Finally, have a supply of personal "business" cards. You can pick up at any office supply store a packet of sheets that will permit printing ten cards to a sheet with an ink-jet printer. It will include templates for setup, or you can search MS Word or Avery's website (http://www.avery.com) for templates. They break apart easily into 100% professional cards. They are for personal use. What you want on them is your name, home address, personal e-mail address, and cell phone number. Carry them with you at all times, and as you engage people about your job search, give them one. You will give one to every interviewer you meet, and you will attach one to every resume you mail.

6.   Draft boilerplate responses.

You will generate many pieces of e-mail and regular mail—thank-you notes of all kinds, e-mail content when responding via Internet job boards, and so on. Each time you create something, save it in a boilerplate <dir> for future reference and use. Be sure to have the filename indicate identify of the document.

7.   Be aware of any limitations on your job search.

Do you have an employment agreement or confidentiality agreement with your current employer? If so, get a copy, read it, and know what limitations it places on where you can work and what you are limited from doing. Are there any trade secret disclosure restrictions? Hopefully it goes without saying that you will not use any of your contacts or current employer resources to the detriment of your current employer—trying to recruit other employees, taking customer lists, and so on.

8.   Don't "cheat" a current employer.

If you are currently employed, you owe your employer all of your time and energy. Truly limit how much job seeking you do on "company time"; do as much as you can on lunch breaks, evenings, and weekends. It's the fair thing to do.

Summary

- You need to get your organizational house in order to conduct a successful job search.

- Document, document, document.

- Have a professional e-mail address.

- Avoid e-mail faux pas.

- Have a business approach to the telephone you use.

- Organize your computer; set up directories (<dir>s).

- Have manila file folders for each potential employer.

- Have a good place to work and keep your job-seeking "stuff."

- Draft boilerplate responses.

- Get a nice professional portfolio, pen, and a supply of personal "business" cards.

- Know of any limitations on your job search.

- Give it all to your current employer; conduct your job search outside of regular job hours.

CHAPTER 5

Basic and Advanced Internet Search Techniques

No doubt you conduct Internet searches frequently, perhaps even several times a day. "Google it" has become a verb as well as an information-gathering process.

This chapter is devoted to helping you be a better and faster Internet researcher and to also show you a few tricks, such as how to see a full LinkedIn profile without getting an "invitation to connect" from the profile holder and how to find *anyone's* business e-mail address. You will also learn to search for posted jobs within specific organizations in a very efficient manner as well as for jobs posted within corporate LinkedIn profiles that you might otherwise not be able to access.

Why would you want to see someone's full LinkedIn profile and to also have his or her business e-mail address? As will be discussed in chapter 8, "Interviewing—The Bridge Between You and Your Next Job," part of your preparation will be to know all you can about who will be interviewing you. Just about the easiest way to do that is to read their full LinkedIn profiles. And if you are trying to establish contacts in one of the target organizations where you think you might want to work, what better way than to mine e-mail addresses of department heads and HR people? You will still mail resumes and cover letters, but you also want e-mail addresses for follow-up purposes.

This chapter will also help you beyond your job-searching activities; you will never search the Internet blindly again, whether you are searching for your dream Corvette, a long-lost college roommate, or a spare shear pin part for a snowblower (as I did!). Share it with your family. You'll get an "aha" moment or two from them!

First, here are a few basics.

Google's "rules" and Boolean "operators"

First of all, this entire chapter applies *only* to searching using Google. There are many other search engines, but Google by far has the edge for the kind of searches you will be doing, so stick to Google for your searches. Besides, the rest of this chapter follows Google's "rules" or algorithms. From Webopedia:

(al'g & rith &m) (n.) A formula or set of steps for solving a particular problem. To be an algorithm, a set of rules must be unambiguous and have a clear stopping point.

We use algorithms every day. For example, a recipe for baking a cake is an algorithm. A series of steps that are unambiguous leads to a perfect cake. Deviate from the recipe and the resulting cake will probably not please the palate!

In the case of a Google search, whatever you type in the Google search window is interpreted by Google according to their algorithms or rules.

Internet searches use one or more of the six Boolean operators to tell a search engine exactly what you want and also to not include results that you don't want.

An example might be in order here. Let's say you are dying to find and buy a 1988 Corvette convertible. You might enter the following into the Google search box:

1988 Corvette convertible

This search yields some 2.6 million results. Yikes! The results include blogs about Corvettes, YouTube videos, companies that sell aftermarket parts, books about Corvettes, and Corvettes for sale all over the country. You want to buy one within 100–150 miles if possible, not one 1,000 miles away, and you don't want to plow through all the extraneous stuff. You just want to see what 1988 Corvette convertibles are for sale near you. By using some of the Boolean "operators", Google's algorithms will narrow the yield considerably, giving you what you want and excluding results you don't want.

Maybe we should back up and define Boolean for you. Suffice it to say, it is a series of functions developed by George Boole in 1854 (waaaaay before the Internet!), and today, the six Boolean operators tell search engines how to process search requests.

I have included the six operators and have **bolded** them for emphasis. That is not necessary when using one or more of these operators:

1. **AND.** By this, I mean the word "and." You never use it; it is implied by Google, so don't waste your time typing "AND" when doing a Google search (not necessarily true if you are using another search engine, but we are only talking about Google searches here). By just having a space between two words, you have instructed Google to find both words on the same page.

2. **"" (Quotes).** You will use quotes around a series of words to find an *exact match* for all of the contents of the quotes *in the same exact order*. Always use for every multiword item. So if we search for "1988 Corvette convertible," we get about 116,000 hits (down from 2.6 million without the quotes!), and almost all of them are about cars for sale. (Keep in mind the number of hits is dynamic – it will change from second to second as the Internet gets new posts!)

    But wait. There is a better way to do this. Enter the following terms:

    1988 "Corvette convertible"

    The number of hits goes up to 370,000. Why? Because the first example required the exact order, so it did not pick up an ad with the text of the ad listed as, "Corvette convertible—1988."

    The order of items in the search doesn't make any difference unless it is in quotes, then it *does* matter. There were two "clauses" in our search:

    1. 1988

    2. "Corvette convertible"—two words in quotes become one clause

    Sidebar: Google doesn't recognize capital letters, except as part of our next operator, so from here on in, in Google searches, use no capital letters: "Corvette" becomes "corvette," and so on.

3.   **OR.** The word OR needs to be used *in all capital letters*. It is the *only* time you will use capital letters in a Google search. All OR commands must be in parentheses (which are our fourth operator), which are used to search for alternative objectives. Suppose your second choice for your Corvette is a 1989 model. You would search by entering this:

(1988 OR 1989) "corvette convertible"

There are two clauses in this search:

1.   (1988 OR 1989)

2.   "corvette convertible"

It makes no difference in what order you list these two clauses. Remember that Google assumes you want to find matches with both of these clauses (the implied AND command is there because you would have a space between the close parentheses after "1989" and before the open quotes in front of "corvette").

You may never run into the situation, but there is a limit of thirty-two words in a Google search string; Google ignores everything beyond the thirty-second word. This search string has four "words" in it. Boolean operators, such as the parentheses, OR, and even the space have no effect on this search string limit. As will see later on, you may have search strings with lots of words in them.

4.   **() (Parentheses).** All OR statements must be in parentheses.

Sidebar: the items you put into a Google search window become a "search string." Our Corvette search, therefore, is done by writing the following search string:

(1988 OR 1989) "corvette convertible"

It is the structure of the search string, including the correct use of one or more of the Boolean operators, that tells Google what you are looking for. From now on, we will refer to creating "search strings."

5.   **- (Minus).** That little symbol is a minus sign and is *not* the same as a dash or hyphen. We use the minus sign to eliminate items from a search. It must be adjacent to the item to be eliminated,

without a space. When used properly, a word that you have excluded with the minus sign *cannot* appear on any page of your search results. If you create your search string in MS Word, Word will make the minus sign into a dash when you hit the space bar to start a new word. You will need to go back and correct it to be a minus sign (which is shorter than a dash). If your minus has become a dash, it will be ignored. So instead of excluding the term, you would have forced it to be included—a critical difference! Let's assume we want our Corvette to *not* be a convertible. Our search string would be the following:

(1988 OR 1989) corvette -convertible

Convertibles will be eliminated from the results of your search; only hardtops and T-tops will be in the search results.

6.   *** (Asterisk).** This symbol is an asterisk and is typically located above the number eight on your keyboard. It is a "wildcard"; it means "fill in the blank." It helps to widen searches. There is always a space before and after it, and *it is always used with quotes.* If we wanted a 1988 red or black convertible and we were open to almost any brand, our search string would be the following:

1988 "(red OR black) * convertible"

The wildcard asterisk permits Google to include in the results such terms as "ford," "dodge," "mustang," "jaguar," and so on. Any time you run a search using an asterisk, you will need to have that clause in quotes. The example above will return you the following results:

1988 red (insert car type) convertible

1988 black (insert car type) convertible

When you are searching in a particular geographic area, you need to include that in your search string. Let's use our Corvette example. Let's assume you live in Philadelphia.

Your search string might be this:

(1988 OR 1989) (red OR black) "corvette convertible" (pennsylvania OR "new jersey" OR delaware)

There is no easy way to search for the areas of the Philadelphia tri-state region that are only close to Philadelphia, so you will just ignore those responses that are too far away in your own judgment. Sometimes you can use local geographic jargon, such as "NEPA" for "northeastern Pennsylvania" or "NOVA" for "northern Virginia," but remember, those results won't show up if no one has listed the car in that manner.

So how does this all figure into doing Google searches during your job search?

Let's assume you are a degreed accountant, currently an accounting manager in Fairfax, Virginia, and seeking a new job as either a controller or accounting manager, depending on the organization. Your search string might be this:

(job OR career OR opportunity OR position) ("accounting manager" OR controller) (nova OR arlington OR fairfax OR alexandria)

You have included local communities and areas in the geographic aspect. You have also included a qualifier identifying a job and a separate OR statement for job title. Take another moment and look at that string. Each separate OR statement is in parentheses, and each has its own theme—job, title, and location. Remember that kindergarten game "one of these things is not like the other"? Do not mix and match within parentheses! Make sure each of your OR statements has similar content.

Sidebar: the first clause for jobs does not include the plural of each word, and it doesn't need it. Google is smart enough to pluralize for you *but* not when you are excluding something with the minus sign. If I wanted the same string but to eliminate those road warrior positions, I would add the following:

-travel -travels -traveling

Remember that if you add Washington DC to your search, put it in quotes—it is a multiword term:

(job OR career OR opportunity OR position) ("accounting manager" OR controller) ("washington dc" OR nova OR arlington OR fairfax OR alexandria)

Bingo—a zillion hits. But wait. It picked up jobs in Arlington, Texas, and Arlington, Massachusetts!

So modify the search string to be this:

(job OR career OR opportunity OR position) ("accounting manager" OR controller) ("washington dc" OR nova OR "arlington (va OR virginia)" OR fairfax OR alexandria)

Much better. You'll get primarily hits of value for you to pursue!

Remember our thirty-two-word rule? This search string has fifteen words in it! Google won't count OR, parentheses, or quotes.

Sidebar: when you have a hit or search result you want to look at, always do so via a right click—"Open in new tab."

When you right click on a Google search result link, this appears:

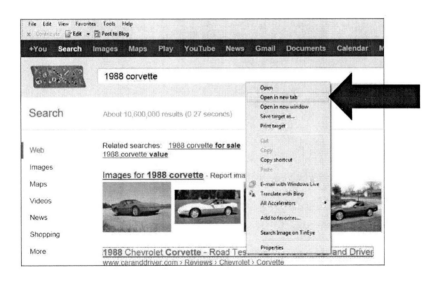

Left click on the highlighted "Open in new tab" of the drop-down menu. This will open the selected search result for you to examine while still keeping your original basic search results intact. If you just left clicked on one of the search results, the result will replace your original search, and sometimes hitting the back arrow won't take you back to where you were.

OK – stop here! This is probably "heavy lifting" for most of you! Go to your PC and play with this a bit. Try some related searches – perhaps for a certain car – or a high school classmate. Get accustomed with creating search strings.

Your accounting manager / controller search will bring up jobs posted by employers, organizations such as trade associations with job boards, the Internet job boards, and staffing services / headhunters. You will also come across folks who want your money to "assist you in your job search." Some career coaches can be of great value; just be sure that you need them, and then vet them carefully before proceeding.

Sidebar: create your search strings in MS Word, and then copy and paste them into the Google search window. Create a MS Word file named "search strings". As you modify the search string to try different searches, save each of them for future use, reference and modification as separate entries in that file. That way you won't lose your search results when you set aside your search efforts to come back later. Just watch what MS Word does to the minus sign—it becomes a dash! You will need to go back and edit it back to a minus sign! The same things happens when we talk in a minute about the field command "site:"; Word will want to capitalize the *s*!

What we have done is create a template for searching for jobs that match what you are looking for in your geographic area:

(job OR career OR opportunity OR position) ("accounting manager" OR controller) ("washington dc" OR nova OR "arlington (va OR virginia)" OR fairfax OR alexandria) =

(job OR career OR opportunity OR position) (job title OR job title) (location OR location OR location)

Just remember that every multiword item must be in quotes.

Be creative, and think like you are placing an ad looking for you. You may have three, four, or five job titles in your search string.

For nurses, include (nurse OR "registered nurse" OR rn) as a job title

For administrative assistants, include ("administrative assistant" OR "admin assistant" OR "executive assistant" OR secretary OR aa)

You know the language of your area of expertise; use as many job titles as might be listed to find someone like you. Just remember to always put them in an OR statement, and if the title has more than one word, it needs to be in quotes. Also remember not to go over the thirty-two-word limit.

You now have new skills to search the Internet and dig out jobs that you might not otherwise come across!

Finding business e-mail addresses

Let's learn how you can find virtually anyone's business e-mail address. Why do you want it?

If a particular organization is on your target list, you need determine to whom you should mail a resume and cover letter. When you mail a cover letter and resume, you want to follow-up within a day or so by e-mail.

Many times regular mail is opened, screened and processed by someone other than your target contact; it may be diverted to HR when you wanted to put it in the hands of a department head or other manager. However, most people process their own e-mail, so the follow-up e-mail will still get your resume and cover letter to your target recipient!

Note that the e-mail will be a replica of your cover letter, which was written to hopefully compel the recipient to read your resume. Write the cover letter as a Word file (to be kept and filed, of course). Then paste it into the body of the e-mail you wish to send. (You may have to adjust the pagination; the pasting process may run together what were separate paragraphs.) That way the recipient can read it easily, and it will also show up in the preview window of his or her e-mail program. End the cover letter e-mail with "I have attached my resume and also a copy of this cover letter." Why also attach the cover letter file? It facilitates being shared internally without having to print the e-mail itself. It also facilitates electronic storage and subsequent retrieval.

Why even send the hard copy resume and cover letter? Because the world of work still operates to a significant degree off of hard copy resumes and cover letters; it is the professional way to initiate a job search communication.

Some organizations list e-mail addresses of staff and department heads on their websites, which makes this task easy. Others, however, do not.

In such a case, you first need to determine the organization's e-mail naming "schema" for e-mail addresses, which is basically how the e-mail is formatted. Here are some examples for a hypothetical William R. Jones, who works at XYZ Company, that you want to e-mail:

bill.jones@xyz.com

william.jones@xyz.com

wr.jones@xyz.com

b.jones@xyz.com

bjones@xyz.com

bill_jones@xyz.com

You've got the picture. Each of these represents a possible standard e-mail naming schema for XYZ Company.

Scour the organization's website to find just one example, usually found in a shareholder's report, a news release, or the president's or chairman's report. Check the "Contact Us" section. Check the site map. If you find that for further information regarding a news release you are to contact j.waterman@xyz.com, now you know the schema and that your contact's e-mail address is probably w.jones@xyz.com. Sometimes there are deviations, but not usually. Now of course William could be Bill, so if your e-mail bounces back, try b.jones@xyz.com.

If you can't find an example to follow, then simply search for this:

"*@xyz.com"

Remember the rules to use the wildcard operator—an asterisk. When looking for an e-mail address, no space should appear before or after the asterisk, and the whole phrase should be in quotes. This is the only time there won't be a space on both sides of the asterisk. Often you will get many results, and you just won't see a single e-mail address easily. Try adding phrases like "press release" or "e-mail me" (both with quotation marks) or "contact" (without quotation marks). Any of these should help bring e-mail results to the top.

In most cases, this will bring up a slew of listings with e-mail addresses in them. Look at a few and you have the schema—and therefore your target's e-mail address!

Sidebar: if you are still having trouble finding even one e-mail address to allow you to decode the schema, it may be different than the company's primary website. This is often done when the company domain is long, but they want short e-mail addresses. Ameriprise Financial has a domain of ameriprise.com but e-mail addresses are from ampf.com. When you can't find an e-mail address using the domain of the main website, just enter in the Google search window the name of the company and the word "e-mail" (without quotation marks), and you should be able to find someone's e-mail address. From there, you can deduce the organization's schema.

Searching within an organization's website

Why would you want to do this? In many cases, internal job openings are posted there—before they are available to the general public. In other words, you have a chance to present your credentials before the general public does. In some cases, they are posted on an organization's website for the entire world to see, but unless you take the time to navigate their website, you won't see it.

Wouldn't it be great to just say to each website of a target organization, "Show me the jobs!"? Well, you can!

In other cases, jobs are posted on corporate LinkedIn profiles, and unless you know which LinkedIn corporate profile to look at, you will never see them. More about this later.

The fact of the matter is that if the job listing is online, you can access it, depending on the organization's firewall. Sometimes you will be researching an organization, and when clicking on a link, you will be asked for a password. Sometimes you can get around this—legally.

You do this by using the "site:" field command. Remember, we are only searching using Google; we are following Google's rules.

This field command starts with the following:

site:xyz.com   Note that we only use part of the URL—we have dropped the "www" and the "http://"

There will never be a space after the colon, and the text is always in lowercase. If you create it in Word, Word will capitalize the *s*, so you will have to go back and edit it to lowercase.

What you are doing is searching the contents of a website, but by using the "site:" command, you are doing so "from the inside"—the website thinks you belong there! Now, if the organization is really security conscious, it will have enhanced the firewall aspects to still ask for passwords to access certain areas, but more often than not, this is not the case.

What are you looking for when you are searching a site? Internal job postings. Add to the field command site: the following:

site:xyz.com (job OR position OR career)

Now to keep me from getting correspondence from some organization's legal department, I am not going to put any real-world examples here, but I did this search, and instead of "xyz.com," I entered the website of a well-known hotel chain headquartered in suburban Washington DC (there is more than one!) and got thousands of hits, including many job postings. Next, I added some local geographic parameters:

site:xyz.com (job OR position OR career) ("washington dc" OR maryland OR virginia)

This search gave me a number of positions local to metro Washington DC.

You want to search for jobs just in a certain area. This is depending on the variety of your experience, of course. But assume you are looking for a position as either an accounting manager or controller.

Then your search string might be this:

site:xyz.com (job OR position OR career) (accountant OR "accounting manager" OR controller) ("washington dc" OR maryland OR virginia)

I did this search—again for that hotel chain—and found twenty-four matches for accounting jobs or jobs in the accounting department.

For some searches, you may not need all of the generic job references—

(career OR position)—if you need more words to describe specific job titles. Always, however include the word "job."

So modify this search string as to your geographic parameters and save it to the "search strings" Word file you have created. Just be sure Word doesn't capitalize the "s" in site. Then substitute for "xyz.com" those organizations on your target list and others as well. Just keep in mind that if those organizations don't post jobs on their websites, you will come up empty-handed.

Keep in mind that only large(er) organizations will usually list job openings on their website, so do this exercise primarily on your target list(s) of local or desired places of employment.

In addition to searching the websites of companies, law firms, and so on, don't overlook trade associations and professional societies. Depending on where you live, you may have the national HQ of a trade association affiliated with your specialty (law/paralegal, accounting/ finance, medicine / health care / nursing / dental, etc.) in your back-yard. If not, perhaps a local chapter is located there. In many cases, firms that are members of these associations and professional societies list their job openings on these websites before releasing them to the general public. So a national organization headquartered a thousand miles away, with a chapter in your state headquartered hundreds of miles away but with a member in your city or town, may have posted a local opening. That is what you are looking for.

Keep in mind that the names of these groups vary, so your first search is to determine who they are and what their website URLs are.

Let's try searching for accounting trade associations or professional societies.

The search string might look like this:

("association of accountants" OR "society of accountants" OR "accounting association") ("washington dc" OR maryland OR virginia)

We get some hits of interest. Then we add asterisks:

("association of * accountants" OR "society of * accountants" OR "accounting association") ("washington dc" OR maryland OR virginia)

By using the asterisk wildcard, we are saying, "Fill in the blank."

One hit we get is Maryland Association of Certified Public Accountants, and we learn that its website URL is http://www.macpa.org. The asterisks brought up "Certified Public."

Just by looking at the site, we find a career center / job board with positions posted! We can skip a further search for jobs because we already found the career center / job board, but we want to see if we can get a member list to selectively contact employers via cover letter and resume.

So we search within the site with the "site:" field command:

site:macpa.org (members OR membership)

And we come up with "members in the news." The membership list itself appears to not be on the website.

But you do have in this example access to a career center / job board as well as several members who may be worthwhile contacting; you will first search for more information about them and their organizations.

If you didn't find a career center / job board, then you might do the following search:

site:macpa.org (job OR position)

Hopefully, you get the idea of how these kinds of searches go!

When you do get a hit of interest—a possible match for your background—*make sure your resume and cover letter "mirrors" the details of the posting's job title and primary responsibilities*. Choose the most important key words in the position listing and *make sure those same identical words* are in both your resume and cover letter. You want your submitted resume and cover letter to look like the absolute match for the posting.

That's a lot of work, you say? Yes, it is. But remember, if you come up empty-handed using the more conventional job-seeking efforts, at least you have an alternative approach. If you are unemployed, looking for work should be treated as a full-time job, and you have the time to do these searches.

Sidebar: another shortcut is to look into the .jobs web domain to scour literally millions of open positions at hundreds of companies. Here's how: simply replace the company you were peering into with the jobs top level domain. While initially confusing, all you need to do is replace "site:xyz.com" with "site:jobs". It used to be that companies would have career sections on their websites, but now many are devoting an entirely different site to their openings. You might find a website like Disney where the jobs are at www.disney.com/careers or at a site with a URL of www.disney.jobs. Since everything here is a job, you can delete the following clause:

(job OR position OR career)

Save this to your Word search string document as well.

See the following example:

site:jobs (accountant OR "accounting manager" OR controller) ("washington dc" OR maryland OR virginia)

Searching within LinkedIn

We are going to explore two ways you will utilize LinkedIn for your job search:

1. Seeing full LinkedIn profiles to review your interviewer's background

2. Searching LinkedIn for jobs listed in corporate LinkedIn members' profiles

As will be discussed in the chapter on interviewing, preparation is the key to success.

That includes knowing something about your interviewer(s). A very easy way to do that is to see their LinkedIn profiles.

Disclaimer: organizations like LinkedIn morph; they change on an almost ongoing basis. So don't be surprised if some of the following screenshots look a little different on your PC. Additionally, since LinkedIn does sell a "recruiter access program" for big bucks to obtain what you will learn below, it is possible that some of these techniques won't work in the future without a different approach. These will be a website associated with this book – look for the URL – and any changes to these procedures will be posted there.

Seeing a basic LinkedIn profiles is easy; you want to see *full* LinkedIn profiles. You can see a full LinkedIn profile of another person in three different ways:

1. You and the person are first-level connections. He or she invited you to connect, and you accepted, or visa-versa.

2. You and the person are connected through a third party; you two are connected at the second level. Both of you are first-level connections with the third party.

3. You use the following search method using the "site:" command.

To see full LinkedIn profiles you must use Google Chrome as your browser. It comes with many PCs. If you don't have it – download and install it – it is free.

To see a full LinkedIn profile, do the following:

Put the following search string in the Google Chrome search box:

site:linkedin.com "first name last name" company

Note that if company name is more than one word, it must be in quotes.

Find the person's result in the list of hits.

Do a right click on it and open using the third option "Open link in incognito window".

The full profile will come up. You may see a request to pay for an upgrade to see even more. The additional information you will see by doing this is minimal, so there is no need to do so.

I suggest you print the profile so you can refer to it just before your interview or whatever contact you will have with him or her. You are going to talk to lots of people, and it is too easy to get confused as to who is who. As part of preparing for your interviews, you will ask, "Who will I be interviewing with? Anyone else?" In most cases, you will be given the names in advance.

What things should you look for on their profiles? Where did they grow up and go to school? Maybe you have something there in common. If so, work it into your prepared remarks, and try to find a way to mention it in the interview (as noted in the interviewing chapter).

Secondly, review their work histories / career paths. Perhaps there is something there you can use as the basis for a question or comment, such as a common employer in the past or common area of employment. Obviously, you don't want to come across as a stalker, so temper your comments and questions to avoid that impression!

Searching LinkedIn for jobs

To search LinkedIn for jobs, use the "site:" field command.

You will, however, have to follow LinkedIn's format for defining geographic areas. LinkedIn has divided the United States into "area" designations with very specific names. Finding the correct geographic area name is where you begin to search for jobs.

1. First, log onto LinkedIn.

2. Then put your city and state into the LinkedIn search window (or the city and state where you want to search for jobs), choose "Companies" from the drop-down window adjacent to the search box. It will look like this:

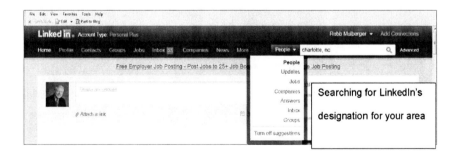

Clicking on the search magnifying glass icon will give you something like this:

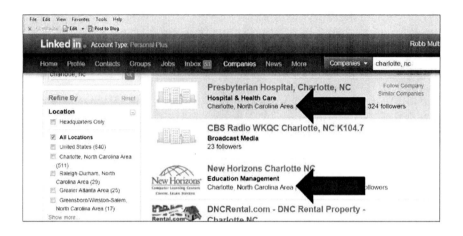

Bingo! You can see that the LinkedIn's designation for Charlotte, North Carolina, is "Charlotte, North Carolina Area."

Off to the left, you can see what it is for Atlanta, Georgia—it will be "Greater Atlanta Area," and for Raleigh-Durham, it is "Raleigh-Durham, North Carolina Area."

For Washington DC, it will be "Washington, D.C. Metro Area." So you can see that the format varies quite a bit.

You must use the correct designation as it appears in your searches.

You are now ready to search for possible jobs of interest, using Google, of course.

Why do we want to search using the field command "site:" when we can search using the "Jobs" classification on the drop-down window adjacent to the search box? Because all you are going to see are the jobs that advertisers have paid to list there. A search I did for accountant jobs in Charlotte, North Carolina, this way yielded just five jobs!

Note that thousands of others have probably seen these ads before you and perhaps applied to fill them.

You want to see the jobs that are listed in the corporate profiles of corporate LinkedIn members. Again, you could do that organization by organization, but wouldn't it be great to say. "Show me all of the jobs in my category in all of the corporate LinkedIn members in my area of interest!"? Well, you can!

Notice in this search string we have added another field command—"inurl:jobs." We are instructing Google to search only the LinkedIn website, only where it says jobs in the URL, only in Charlotte, North Carolina, and only for an accountant or controller position.

The search string looks like this:

site:linkedin.com inurl:jobs "Charlotte, North Carolina Area" (accountant OR controller)

This yielded 954 hits!

Results will vary second by second because the Internet is so dynamic, but this is a gold mine of opportunities to search!

Remember to open results of interest with a right click to open a new tab to preserve your original search window.

As you review results, note that at the bottom of many listings this will appear: "People Who Viewed This Job Also Viewed."

This is followed by a number of other corporate job listings!

Your template to search LinkedIn for job listings is this:

site:linkedin.com inurl:jobs "LinkedIn's specific geographic area" (job title OR job title OR job title)

Since you are doing this in Google, remember Google's rules:

1. Ensure that there is a lowercase "s" in the "site:" command.

2. Multiword entries must be in quotes.

3. Alternative targets use the OR command in parentheses.

Happy searching!

Summary

- Know how to use the six Boolean operators.

- Know Google's rules, and only search using Google.

- Open search results in a new tab.

- Create a Word file, and add to it all of your search strings. Be creative as you write search strings; try different approaches.

- Know how to find e-mail addresses.

- Know how to search within an organization's website.

- Know how to see the full LinkedIn profiles of the people you are going to be meeting and talking to.

- Know how to search for jobs in corporate LinkedIn profiles in your target area.

There are entire courses built around using Boolean techniques to search online, and this is just a thin slice of a big pie. I participated in just such a class taught by Peter Leffkowitz's team at the Morgan Consulting Group (www.morgancg.com). It was in that class that I learned these techniques to in turn train recruiters in my organization. The Morgan team would remind you of a couple of things:

1. Practice! This is one of those times when it is okay to go play on the Internet.

2. Less is more. A huge, complicated search string that has only one exact perfect-match job for you won't help. An expansive search where you see nineteen thousand job postings also will not help. You will spend all day clicking "Apply Now."

3. Morgan trains recruiters to find people using very similar techniques, so if you want to be found by a recruiter, you are getting a glimpse into their psychology. Now reverse engineer your LinkedIn profile so they can find you. That makes for the easiest job search ever.

CHAPTER 6

How to Best Use a Staffing Service Company / Headhunter

Staffing service firms come in all shapes and sizes but basically fall into four categories:

1. Employment agency

These firms find jobs for people and may charge a fee to the job seeker. There are fewer and fewer of these types of firms, and they are usually found in smaller towns and cities. If an employment agency wants to charge you a fee, you should decline and not work with them. To a great extent, their function has been assumed by contingency search firms.

2. Contingency search firm

They find potential employees for organizations with positions to fill. They are only paid by the employer when they are successful in doing so (their fee is *contingent* upon the employer hiring a candidate referred by the contingency search firm). They typically fill positions from entry level up to the low six figures in salary ($100,000+). Sometimes referred to as "direct hire" firms.

3. Retained search firm

They also find potential employees for organizations with positions to fill but are paid regardless; they are *retained* to find candidates for the position. Their fee is not contingent upon a candidate being hired; they are paid a retainer fee to find candidates. They typically are retained to fill highly specialized and senior-level positions with salary levels in the six-figure range and even into the seven-figure range ($1 million+).

4.   Temporary staffing services

These firms send "temps" to work at the clients' place of business. The "temp" is the bona fide employee of the temporary help service, with all of the statutory protections and rights of any employee of any organization in the United States. Today's temporary workers include virtually every job category and title, including lawyers, accountants, doctors, and professionals of all kinds at all levels.

Many staffing service firms provide both contingency search and temporary staffing services.

Temporary jobs are excellent ways to explore new opportunities, provide employment during summer vacations for students and teachers, and help facilitate getting back into the job market for those that have not worked for some time. For many professionals (nurses, high-end IT types, doctors, etc.), it is the preferred type of employment due to the diversity of assignments, flexibility of work duration and location, helping to stay on top of technology, and so on.

Working as a temporary worker is also the pathway to a full-time career position for entry-level positions. Referred to as "temp to hire," it is the process of an employer hiring a person to fill a full-time career position via a "tryout" method versus the traditional interviewing selection method. More about that later.

Most probably, you will utilize the services of a search firm (contingency or retained) and/or a temporary help service in your search for employment. Using them can provide exposure to many more opportunities than you can find on your own—and anonymously at first, protecting the fact that you are looking for another job if you are currently employed.

Regardless of the nature of the staffing service firm you work with, *you should never, ever pay a placement fee or sign a contract of any kind.* Historically, employment agencies have often asked applicants to do so since it is the applicant who is responsible for their fee. Some less-than-scrupulous contingency search firms have asked applicants to sign an agreement to reimburse the staffing firm for the placement fee if for some reason the staffing firm needs to make a refund back to the employer. Don't ever sign such an agreement.

The rest of this chapter will focus on contingency and retained search firms as well as temporary staffing services. Remember, many staffing service firms provide both search and temporary staffing services. We will refer to them for brevity as "staffing services."

Some other facts about staffing services

1. Many specialize in a particular discipline or area of focus. This can be by function, the most common being the following:

    - Accounting and finance

    - Legal

    - Health care and medical

    - Technical and engineering

    - IT

    - Office administration

    Staffing services can specialize by industry, such as the following:

    - Chemical

    - Automotive

    - Education and academia

    - Aeronautical

    - Marine

    This type of specialization will be confined to those positions unique to those industries; even though all of these industries employ accountants, staffing services that specialize in one of these and similar will not typically place accountants—rather they will place the engineers, technicians, and other specialists unique to those industries.

    Some staffing services will cover a number of areas of specialization in an effort to be a diversified staffing service, offering a "full-service" approach to employers. In those cases, it is common to find that certain staff members will focus in one specialty (such as health care and medical) while other staff members will focus on another (such as accounting and finance).

What this means to you is that before your submit your resume to a staffing service or take steps to register with one or more of them, you need to know if they work in the area where your next job will be. A firm that specializes in the health care and medical arena will have zero interest in the resume of an accountant. Remember, the mission of these firms is to fill specific job openings within their client companies. A health care and medical staffing service does not have job openings that match a job-seeking accountant!

2.   Staffing services work for employers that have positions to be filled. Staffing services work on behalf of both candidates and employers, but it is the employer with a need that institutes the process whereby a hire eventually takes place. This is logical since it is the employer who pays the placement fee.

While staffing services that specialize in your area will welcome your resume, it will result in immediate activity only if they have a current search assignment in process that calls for someone like you or they know of a standing need within one of their client companies.

In those instances where a staffing service / recruiter has a strong and regular working relationship with an employer who has ongoing needs in your job area, the fact that you have surfaced as a candidate may well be presented anonymously to that employer as soon as your resume hits the recruiter's desk. If there is broad interest on the employer's part, the recruiter will begin the process of working with you to see if there is a match and interest on your part.

Regardless, you want to register with selected staffing services sooner rather than later. That way when a job opening that is a match does occur, your name will surface when the staffing service does a search of their database.

3.   Their reputation is their "stock-in-trade," which means they have to be trusted by their employers/clients to have done a thorough

job of screening the candidates they refer to them for interview. Which means you need to be 100% truthful with regard to your resume and your interview with them. The staffing service will be checking your references and depending on the type of job they are filling perhaps administering some skill tests—and maybe some other tests as well.

Being 100% truthful also entails letting your staffing service recruiter know of any plans that would prevent you from being able to begin a full-time career-oriented position with expectations of being there for the long run. That means do not hide the fact that you will be moving to Germany in seven months to get married or that your plan is to return to school in a year.

4. You are expected to be 100% reliable. That means you show up to interview on time and dressed for business. It also means you check e-mail several times a day and return all calls promptly. Often their clients have a small window of time available for interviews, and if the staffing service can't contact you to schedule an interview, you may well lose a chance to be in the running.

    Keep in mind that the staffing service and your recruiter are the gatekeepers to their client base; treat them exactly as you would an employer.

How do you select which staffing service to work with?

Just as in any business, there are good ones, great ones, and some not-so-good ones.

1. Start with those you have worked with successfully in the past. If this is not an option, then start with those recommended by people whose judgment you respect.

2. Select those that are members of the American Staffing Association (ASA). The ASA website (www.americanstaffing.net) lists them all and cross-references their areas of specialization and location. ASA member firms subscribe to a code of ethics and tend to be the leading staffing services in their town or city.

3. Look also for firms that are members of their local staffing services associations. The website of a local staffing service association will

list member firms by specialty and location. You can find those local staffing service associations listed on the ASA website.

4.   As you scan the online job boards and classified ads, note which staffing services ads you see in your job search area and especially those that impress you with their content and "look." If your background is in an area served by specialty publications, such as law, accounting, human resources, and so on, review the "help wanted" advertising sections in those publications. Almost without fail, those staffing service ads will be placed by firms that specialize in that arena.

5.   Select two to three staffing services based upon all of this research, and make a phone call to each of them, either asking to speak to a specific recruiter based upon an ad or just any recruiter. You want to "interview" them to determine their competency in your areas of expertise. Talk to the recruiter from a prepared script:

> Hello. My name is Harry Smith, and I am an accounting /finance professional in the process of finding a new job. I noted your firm's advertising for (specific position you saw advertised or accounting and finance positions in the past). Tell me a little about the kinds of jobs you are filling these days.

Listen carefully. You are looking for someone who clearly is able to explain his or her firm's area of staffing expertise. Do you sense warmth and sincerity over the phone? Ask questions as necessary to find out:

- How long have you been a recruiter? How long has your firm been in business?

- How large is your staff? (You want to avoid one- or two-person firms; there is just not enough depth to serve both employers and candidates.)

- How many (your desired job title in your next job) positions have you filled in the last three months? Last six months? Last year?

- If I chose to work with you and your firm, what is the process?

- Is your firm a member of the American Staffing Association?

6. From there, proceed to submit your resume, visit with them, and go through the process with those firms you feel can be of service to you.

Should you register with more than one staffing service?

Yes, but not more than two or three. You don't want every staffing service in town out flogging your credentials and resume all about, especially if you are currently employed and trying to keep your job search 100% confidential from your current employer. If your experience with one of those selected is not favorable, feel free to cease working with that firm, and begin the process with another staffing service.

The exception to this is if you are unemployed and willing to work as a temp until you find a full-time career position. Then you want to register with three to five temporary staffing firms to give you broad exposure to available assignments. This is where registering with a staffing service with strong competency in both temporary staffing and contingency searching can be highly advantageous for obvious reasons.

What are your responsibilities when working with a staffing service?

We have talked about being 100% upfront and honest with them, being reliable, and being almost instantly available to discuss opportunities as they arise. For them to be as successful as possible in placing you in a job you will find exciting and challenging, there are a few more things you need to do.

1. Be reasonable. Imagine you are buying a house or renting an apartment. You would like lots of open space, a fireplace, the most modern of kitchens and bathrooms, nine-foot ceilings with crown molding, and finally, a water view. Good luck. Not gonna happen. Same thing with finding a job with lots of money, short commute, the best boss on the planet, the nicest facility ever, generous benefit plan, and pizza parties every Friday afternoon. Again, not gonna happen!

    A staffing service can't create jobs; they can only refer you to those that they have been asked to fill and which you are both qualified for and interested in. You need to have reasonable parameters regarding the criteria that are the most important to you—usually money, commuting distance/time, and opportunities for advancement.

Depending on where you live, a ten-minute commute is probably not possible, so don't make that a must for your staffing service to achieve. Give the staffing service the absolutes (e.g., minimum salary of $47,000, and no more than an hour commute under normal circumstances), and be flexible on the other issues. And even on those absolutes, be flexible. Would you accept the job at $46,500? Think it through, and be prepared to respond.

2. Evaluate opportunities as they develop. If discussions with a spouse or significant other will be part of the formula of accepting or rejecting a job offer, discuss the pros and cons with him or her as the interviews develop. Discuss the pros and cons with your recruiter as well. When an offer comes through, you want to be in position to do one last evaluation and then decide—ideally, when the offer is made but no later than a day after.

Your recruiter will be in a negotiating mode with the employer, regarding compensation, start date, and any adjustments to benefits as things begin to jell toward an offer. In fact, this negotiation on your behalf is one of the advantages of using a staffing service; they can do so much more easily than you could on your own. In many cases, your recruiter will be the one to extend the offer to you on behalf of the employer, and you will accept or reject the offer to your recruiter.

3. Be upfront about potential job offers as they begin to come together. It will do you no good to lead a recruiter on (and therefore an employer) regarding being very interested about an opportunity and then rejecting it at the eleventh hour on the basis of a heretofore known factor (commute—it is what it is; money—the offer is within your range; etc.). Tell your recruiter if you expect an offer soon from an employer you have been in direct contact with or through another staffing service. Your recruiter can use this information to move toward an offer from those employers he or she has been working with on your behalf.

What is this thing called "temp to hire"?

Traditional hiring practices call for extending a job offer as a result of an interviewing process, the checking of references, perhaps some skill testing, and other testing and evaluation processes. This entire chain of events is designed to find out how you will perform in all regards before making a commitment to you in the form of a job offer. A hiring mistake is costly in terms of lost momentum to start over again, lost productivity, the impact on coworkers and customers, and finally, the negative impact on a firm's unemployment tax experience rating. In our litigious society, it is not the hiring process that worries HR professionals, managers, and CEOs. It is the unhiring process—the need to terminate an employee. Unjust termination lawsuits can cost organizations huge sums and be highly disruptive—hence the need for firms to hire very carefully with a secondary mission to screen out potential problem employees.

For certain categories of jobs, the solution to this dilemma is "temp to hire" (sometimes called "temp to perm"). For positions with little customer contact, little investment in training, and where turnover is not highly disruptive, more and more employers have turned to temp to hire, especially for entry-level jobs. It is a means of hiring a full-time career employee based on a tryout process versus a selection process. The employer asks the staffing service to find a person to fill the position as a temp for a certain period of time, usually ranging from ten weeks to ninety days. During that time, the temp on assignment will be evaluated as to performance in all regards, and a decision will be made whether or not to extend an offer to become an employee of the organization. If performance, behavior, and the like do not meet the criteria to be offered a job on the organization's payroll, the staffing service will be so notified, the temp will be taken off the assignment, and the staffing service will send another temp on assignment to start the process over again. Filling a full-time position through this approach shifts the employer-employee relationship to the staffing service, and the individual involved knows that he or she is working as a temp during the tryout period.

Because of the difficulty in evaluating work performance of entry-level people (little or no previous work experience to use as a guideline), temp to hire has become the preferred method for many employers to fill entry-level positions.

From your perspective, it is a great way to evaluate a job and organization without making a firm commitment on your part; it is a tryout for both parties.

What do you do when a headhunter calls?

As you move up through your career path, it will become more and more common to get calls from recruiters—headhunters. Staffing firms and recruiters get their candidates through a variety of means, including cold calls placed to potential candidates.

Typically, such a call will go like this:

"Susan, this is Frank Williams calling. I am a recruiter with a unique opportunity I think you might find of interest. Do you have a moment to talk?"

Or

"Susan, this is Frank Williams calling. I have been asked by one of Midland City's finest organizations to fill a position that I think may be of interest to you. Do you have a moment to talk?"

It makes sense for you to talk to the recruiter. It never hurts to be in several recruitment firms' databases. Listen to what the recruiter has to say. If it is still of interest, ask the questions detailed previously in this chapter to establish the credentials of the staffing service's / headhunter's firm and the recruiters themselves.

Proceed as you see fit from there.

"Candidate" versus "applicant"

For staffing firm professionals, there is a difference between a "candidate" and an "applicant," and their objective is to decide which of the two is the person in front of them or on the phone during an initial interview.

Candidates are people who are committed to making job changes. Maybe not right away, maybe not next month, but by a certain target date, they want to be in other jobs. They are going to make those job changes for all the right reasons; they want to further their careers when they have hit dead ends; their employers are moving some distance away, and they don't want to make the move; their firms have been acquired, and they have reasonably concluded that they may the losers in the competition for the one job that was two before the acquisition. Candidates will work with their recruiters and will do all the positive things discussed in this chapter.

Applicants are people who will change jobs—maybe—if the right thing comes along. They are not, however, committed to making changes in their employment within a certain time frame. Oftentimes, to them jobs are just that—not part of career paths and plans. They may want to shop to "see what is out there," they may want to "see what I am worth on the job market." Their lack of commitment makes them not very desirable to the staffing firm or recruiter. That lack of commitment often translates to not showing up for interviews and turning down offers, which in turn truly puts the staffing firm in hot water with their employer client.

Don't be an applicant; be a candidate, or don't bother throwing your hat in the ring! Based upon the fact that the past predicts the future, acting like an applicant is a surefire way to be purged from a staffing service's database.

My firm, NRI Staffing Resources of Washington DC, processes thousands of applications every year—people that want either temporary jobs or permanent full-time career positions. We treat each and every one of them in a professional and effective manner. After all, each of them represents potential revenue for NRI. Some of them, however, are simply "unworkable." There are several reasons for this:

- When told that they will have to submit to a drug test, some asked to go to the restroom and never came back. (Hmm, I wonder why?)

- Our self-entry application process asks about criminal convictions. When we run a criminal background check, oftentimes the results that come back are very different than what the applicants indicated when they completed their applications. In some cases, the results of a criminal background can adversely impact the doors that are open for employment. Of course, it depends on the specifics and how long ago the convictions took place.

- The results of reference checks should reflect the information that was gathered during our in-office initial interview. When this is not the case, we dig in to reconcile the discrepancies and determine the truth. Sometime the results disqualify the individual from consideration.

These examples are all reflective of past mistakes or lapses in judgment. What also hurts our ability to assist these people to find jobs are behavioral issues starting with the time they contacted us.

- Some are late for their initial interviews with us and then late again for an interview with prospective employers. In both cases, a plausible excuse was not given. These candidates then wondered why we declined to work with them any more. (The past predicts the future, that's why!)

- For others, getting responses to voice mails or e-mails is slow and unreliable; opportunities are lost while waiting to hear back from them.

- Some will not accept "we will call when we have something for you" and instead call their recruiters almost daily.

- Many have a "tude"—an "in-your-face" attitude. They are difficult people to work with, sullen and angry that they are unemployed or that we can't get them the perfect job. They are unreasonable in their salary demands. The "lightbulb never goes on" when we point out the discrepancies between their skill test scores, references, experience and their minimum salary levels.

  Furthermore, they are belligerent when we can't secure interviews for them. We try to explain that while they may have made $67,000 at their last job, it was because they were there for seventeen years, and they enjoyed a phenomenon called salary creep—getting a raise every year beyond both cost of living and market standards. They didn't want to hear that the going salary for their job, experience, and so on was in the $47,000–$50,000 range. They just didn't get it!

We have all met these folks. They just wear you down, so when repeated counseling fails to correct these factors to make them job placeable, we choose to no longer work with them. Organizations that ask staffing services to fill professional-level jobs—career or temp—

don't want people with an "attitude" and related problems. Employers can find problematic people on their own; they expect a staffing services firm to find them temps and candidates that are of a higher caliber for full-time jobs.

Compare that to the candidates we refer to that "walk on water":

- Great attitude, gracious, appreciative, cooperative

- Reasonable as to salary and other criteria of the jobs they were seeking; understand how the world of employment works

- 100% reliable; the ones that make it to an interview despite the January snowstorm

- Return calls and e-mails very promptly

For these people, we pull out all the stops because not only are they easy to work with, but those attributes will make them very employable in the eyes of our clients/employers. So in addition to the difference between applicants and candidates, be aware of the impact of behavior and "baggage" that will either aid or hurt your chances of a staffing service finding you a job.

Summary

- Staffing services can provide exposure to many more opportunities than you can on your own and anonymously at first—protecting the fact that you are looking for another job.

- Carefully choose which firm(s) you will use based upon their areas of expertise and specialization; "interview" the firms you are considering by asking questions as to their competency in your areas of expertise.

- Never sign any contract or agree to pay any amount.

- Staffing services can negotiate for you better than you can for yourself.

- Temp to hire is often the path to a full-time job, especially for entry-level jobs.

- Treat headhunters that cold call you with respect; it is advantageous to be in their databases once you have qualified them.

- Be sensitive to a staffing service's expectations; be a candidate, not an applicant!

CHAPTER 7

Your Resume: The Key to Your Next Job—Better Get it Right!

If you sent your resume to your uncle Fred, president of the family business, no matter how bad it was, he would still invite you to come in for an interview. Family ties count.

Most of the time, however, your resume is read by a series of strangers. These readers briefly scan a resume for a few seconds to a minute to see which of 3 piles it goes into:

• No

• Maybe

• Yes

Those in the "Yes" pile are the only ones studied to see if they meet enough of the job criteria to merit further consideration. Only if there aren't any "Yes" resumes are the "Maybe" resumes reviewed in any detail. And from there comes the call or e-mail inviting a candidate for an interview.

And now technology enters the picture. More and more frequently, especially with larger organizations, resumes are processed by scanners. Resumes are scanned for specific words, phrases and comparing content against the job description. Therefore, your resume must "mirror" the job description to the greatest extent possible. Make sure the job title and primary responsibilities are—word for word—included in your resume and cover letter. Choose the most important key words in the position listing and make sure those *identical words* are featured in your resume, including in the lead-in "Summary of

Experience and Accomplishments" statement. Do the same for the cover letter. Without those key words, your resume may not make even the preliminary cut!

And while we are on the subject of resumes being processed by scanners, note that the chances are very high that resumes submitted to larger organizations via their website are automatically headed to the scanner. Accordingly, whenever possible, bypass submitting your resume via a website and rather find a way to send it directly to a person by regular mail or email.

Therefore, your resume is the key that begins to open the door. I have probably seen tens of thousands of resumes over the past forty years, and indeed, some of them have been "doozies". Many have been riddled with typos, have been a copy of a copy of a copy (which somewhere along the way got on the copy machine crooked), have had a circular coffee cup stain, have been unreadable for a variety of grammatical and syntax errors, don't have contact information included—how did that get by the sender?—and so on.

The one that really stands out in the outlandish category was from the self-proclaimed "King of Sales"! Had a large picture printed on the first page of the resume of a man on a throne—in an ermine robe of sorts and with a crown on his head. Surrounding him was his family dressed in medieval attire! Yikes! What was he thinking?

Well, to add some perspective to how you should *not* prepare your resume read on!

To have your resume *effectively eliminate you* from ever getting that telephone call or e-mail to discuss your credentials, follow these time-tested rules:

1. Tell it all. Go back fifteen years or more to include every job in great detail. So what if it goes on for four or five pages? It's all important stuff, right?

Wrong! The resumes that make it to the "Yes" pile have these qualities:

• Reader friendly—*concise* and easy to read

• Focused—allows the reader to quickly grasp *current capabilities*

- "Cuts to the chase"—tells what the candidate has *most recently* accomplished

2.   Use as many pages as you need.

Wrong! Recruiters don't want to plow through a three-, four-, or five-page resume. Even with twenty-plus years of varied experience, two pages is sufficient to tell your story. Remember, the purpose of the resume is to tell the reader why you should be interviewed.

3.   Write it with no objective critique by others. After all, who knows you better than you!

Wrong! You have very little objectivity when it comes to your own resume. Have someone else, and preferably several other people, read and critique your resume. Ask them specifically to look for the "who cares" and "so what" statements that can creep into resumes such as a statement that you were active in the Boy's Club in your hometown some ten years ago. So what! That has nothing to do with your ability to do the controller job you are seeking. But if you were president of that Boy's Club and helped double its endowment, now that would be worth mentioning.

Don't have your resume professionally written. You don't need to spend the $$ to do so if you follow these guidelines.

4.   List activities instead of results and accomplishments.

Wrong! The reader is looking to see what you have accomplished and the results you brought to previous positions. Terms such as "responsible for" and "coordinated" can't stand alone without measurable results. Your resume needs to tell "what happened because you were there."

Far too many resumes are full of "activity statements." Better to have two statements of achievement of results than ten activity statements.

5.   Use creativity—colored paper and inks. Include a photo, use fancy, eye-catching graphics. Maybe use a gimmick, such as sending your resume in a file folder with your name on the tab. Perhaps have it folded like a brochure or put into a binder.

Wrong! This isn't a graphics competition. Remember, your resume should be "reader friendly"! Besides, colored paper and ink don't photocopy well.

Include a photo? Why? Even if you look like a movie star, your picture won't increase your odds of receiving that phone call or e-mail for an initial interview.

Fancy presentations? If your resume leads to an interview, the employer will want to make photocopies to distribute internally. Your resume needs to be "photocopy friendly."

If you are interviewing for a creative position, have a portfolio of your work. That is the place to show your stuff.

6.   Start with an "Objective" statement listings the things you want in your next job.

Wrong! With all due respect, initially, who cares what you want? The resume reader is only interested in whether you are or are not qualified for the position he or she is trying to fill. The time for your interests and objectives to surface is during interviews and when it comes time to accept or decline the offer.

You should, however, begin your resume with a "Summary of Experience and Accomplishments" statement. Be careful to keep it objective, and be sure it includes factual results and accomplishments, not superlatives. See examples in the sample resumes below.

7.   Don't make a cover letter part of your resume submission.

Wrong! A cover letter (one page maximum) is a must, and its objective is to tell the recipient why he or she should read your resume. It paints the overall picture of who you are and why you are submitting your resume. The cover letter personalizes your resume; it should be tailored to the organization to which it is being sent and specifically for the position you wish to interview for. If responding to an ad or job posting, have your cover letter "mirror" the language in the ad or posting.

I estimate that over half the resumes I have reviewed over the years have not included a cover letter. Not having a cover letter forces the reader to start reading without knowing, generally, what he or she is about to read.

The letter should be businesslike. Don't start it with "Good Morning" or anything other than a proper business greeting.

Avoid overkill. Don't include phrases such as "Are you looking for a superstar?" or "I'm a one-of-a-kind take-charge person." Let your accomplishments and what you have done speak for you.

Your cover letter and envelope should be on paper stock that matches your resume. There are many sources for matching paper and envelope. Just be sure it is white and of a good quality (not copier paper).

E-mailed resumes have a unique cover letter challenge. Unlike normal mail where the cover letter is the top sheet—and hence the first to be read—how do you do this with an e-mailed resume?

Simple. Make the cover letter the text of your e-mail and then also submit it as an MS Word attachment. Write it in Word, and then paste it into the body of the e-mail. Your resume of course, is the second Word attachment. In both cases, the file names should be "yourname-cover-letter-org.doc" and "yourname-resume-org.doc". The "org" is the name of the employer you are submitting to and can be abbreviated. Naming the files that way to enables them to be filed and retrieved easily—both by you and the organization—as well as differentiating between your resume and the cover letter. You need to have the organization's name as part of the file name, since each cover letter will have a unique salutation and may have differences in content (as might be the case with your resume).

End the cover letter e-mail with "I have attached my resume and also a copy of this cover letter." Why also attach the cover letter file? It facilitates being printed to be shared internally without having to print the e-mail itself.

8. Use the same resume and cover letter every time you submit your resume.

Wrong! Each position you apply for is unique as are the organizations you seek to work for. Most of the customizing is in the cover letter, but you will also revise the resume to match the circumstances.

For example, let's assume you are a degreed accountant with significant experience as an accounting manager and controller. Your resume for a job as a VP of finance will stress your management experience while your resume for a job as a controller will stress your hands-on experience generating financial statements.

Sidebar—Really Important: if you are responding to a specific position, *every resume and cover letter* needs to "mirror" the job listing! It is becoming more common for resumes to be processed via scanning and key word search. As noted before, without those key words, your resume may not make even the preliminary cut!

9.   Write your resume in the third person.

Wrong! Do you talk about yourself in the third person? "Ms. Jones increased output and productivity by 40%" versus "I achieved a 40% increase …"

Of course you don't! Then don't write that way.

10.   Include personal information, such as hobbies, names and number of children, marital status, social organizations and affiliations, and so on.

Wrong again! This information is not necessary, takes up space, and is just that much more detail the reader has to read and digest.

Wrapping up this list - is your resume clean of <u>all</u> of these errors? Good for you! You might be surprised as to how many resumes we see that include one or more of these resume blunders!

Other resume guidelines

1.   Don't include references or the statement "References upon request."

It just takes up space, and generally, the organization is not going to rely upon who you list as references. They will want to talk to former bosses and possibly coworkers and will ask for that contact information at an appropriate time.

At the same time, however, if you have a relatively recent (five years or less) letter of commendation from a former boss that talks in glowing terms of an achievement or accomplishment, make copies of it to present during the interview process. Do the same for the written text accompanying an award. If you worked for a boss that is now out of the country or otherwise very difficult to reach, take the time to get him or her to write something glowing about you that you can present during the interview (but not sooner).

2.   Don't ever submit a resume that is a copy of a copy.

You lose clarity. Every resume you mail should be an original printed one or a photocopy of an original on a high-quality copy machine. And if you do copy it, be sure it is straight on the copier. I can't begin to tell you how many people mail resumes that are crooked on the page! It speaks of sloppiness.

3.   Don't clutter your resume with extra "stuff."

Again, keep it reader friendly. Don't submit letters of recommendation you have solicited, the brochure that you wrote, or other literature that mentions you by name unless it is specifically requested. If you have published a book or article, mention that in your resume

4.   Use a chronological format.

There are essentially two different resume formats: chronological and functional. Look at the examples at the end of this chapter; these are chronological resume. Each position is listed in sequence, starting with the most current position and working backward. It is easy to understand the person's career path. You don't need complete sentences—bulleted phrases are fine; just tell the story. A chronological resume like this is the preferred format; avoid the functional format that details functions performed, skill sets, and areas of work responsibility but does not do so by employer or date. It is confusing and makes it difficult to follow a career path.

5.   Decide on the proper amount of detail for each position listed on your resume

Notice the information listed about each employer. Leave out specific addresses or telephone numbers.

- Notice the amount of information about each position is weighted so that the more recent position has more space devoted to it than previous positions.

- A good rule of thumb is to detail the last three jobs or go back ten years, whichever is greater. Information about positions before ten years ago or three positions back should just be listed with no details provided. Just list employer, job title, and city/state of the position.

6.   Provide the proper content.

An effective resume answers some basic questions. Write your resume to answer the following:

- What do you do for a living? If your job title is confusing or could be misleading, be sure to clarify. Keep it brief, but be specific.

- What have you accomplished? Did you do anything exemplary?

- What specific experience do you have? Have you chaired a committee? Were you responsible for installing a new computer system? What happened successfully because you were there in the job? Detail this information briefly.

7.   Limit the use of graphics and formatting

Note that the use of graphics is limited to bold, bullets, and underlining

8.   Make sure your resume is consistent with other available information about you such as your LinkedIn profile.

They need to match (not be in conflict); make sure such online profiles are up to date.

9.   Be truthful at all times about all things.

There are two major ways to not be truthful. Both are guaranteed to put you, at the very least, in the worst possible light. In many cases, one or the other will result in your immediately being eliminated from consideration (or terminated if hired!).

Don't make errors of omission, such as hiding gaps in work history or otherwise not revealing information that the interviewer is seeking. If you were unemployed for a period of time, reveal that, and make sure you explain it in your cover letter (briefly). You don't have to bare your soul, and you don't have to provide details that might cast you in a bad light, but you do have to be honest.

Don't make errors of commission. This is even worse. This is claiming a degree you don't have, a job title you didn't have, or accomplishments that weren't yours. Remember, your references will be checked, unearthing discrepancies in degrees claimed, schools attended, job titles claimed, areas of responsibility claimed, and so on. A significant number of resumes have errors of omission and, more commonly, errors of commission—lying on a resume.

What are the consequences? Just ask George O'Leary or Ronnie Few. Who? George O'Leary's dream job was to be Notre Dame's head football coach. And he was—for five days in 2001. He claimed to have a master's degree and to have played college football for three years, but both of these claims were not true. Bye-bye, George. Ronnie Few was Washington DC's fire chief beginning in 2000 for twenty-two months, until it was discovered that he lied about his professional and educational achievements in his resume. Bye-bye, Ronnie. It is amazing how many high profile people have fallen from grace due to lying on their resume! To George and Ronnie we can also add former Yahoo CEO Scott Thompson…and the list goes on!

Your resume is 100% within your control! If there is some thing on it that isn't true and accurate – only you are to blame. Need we say more?

Get to work on that resume and refer to the samples that follow.

Summary

- Remember our objectives:

    - The cover letter—the objective is to get someone to read your resume

    - The Resume the objective is to obtain an interview, either by phone or in person

    - The interview—the ultimate objective of the resume and cover letter!

- Avoid the ten surefire resume mistakes that can only hurt your chances.

- Observe the guidelines offered.

- Always, always be truthful on your resume and cover letter.

- Review the sample resumes and cover letters, and begin creating yours. Be sure to get others to critique it.

Susan T. Someone, CPA
1234 King Street, Alexandria, VA 22314
(703) 123-4567 (Home) (703) 987-6543 (Cell)
susancpa888@gmail.com

Summary of Experience and Accomplishments – 12 years of accounting experience, including 5 years of public accounting. Account management responsibility for several SEC-reporting clients. Supervise audit teams. Specialize in trade association accounting procedures and software, including unique tax and foundation issues. Featured speaker at trade association CFO seminars.

Employment History –

Really Great CPA Firm, CPAs – Vienna, VA
June 2004–Present   Senior Associate
- My audit teams completed all work ahead of target dates and to client satisfaction.
- Brought in two new audit clients due to referrals from existing clients and presentations make.
- A member of the new business presentation team; three additional new audit clients added in 2008.
- Guided client through conversion from C Corp to Sub-S status.
- Retained by client to install new accounting system, including MAS 90 software.
- Presenter to the 2012 Association of Finance Professionals conference in Philadelphia.

Really Nice Trade Association – Alexandria, VA
April 2002–June 2004 Controller
- Converted accounting software system—on time and under budget.
- Implemented associate member program for international firms.
- Appointed to attend and participate in board of directors meetings.
- Combined several internal positions through automation and job engineering.
- Performed audit work on association foundation and PAC.

December 1999–April 2002   Staff Accountant
- Supervised all nondues revenue programs; increased revenue by 16%.
- Converted accounting software system—on time and under budget.
- Performed internal audits; liaison to outside auditing firm.

<u>Very Small Company</u> – McLean, VA
July 1987–December 1999   Staff Accountant
- Generated internal financial statements.
- Processed A/R and A/P.
- Created aging reports with dialogue for collection efforts.

Education –
BS – Business Administration (Accounting) – 3.8 GPA – Penn State University, University Park, PA.
Vice President – Future Financiers Club

Susan T. Someone, CPA
1234 King Street, Alexandria, VA 22314
(703) 123-4567 (Home) (703) 987-6543 (Cell)
susancpa888@gmail.com

Mr. William J Harris   Date

Managing Partner

XYZ National Accounting Firm

1633 M Street NW Suite 900

Washington, DC 20006

Dear Mr. Harris:

I am writing in regard to your published position on your website for senior auditor.

As can be seen on my enclosed resume, I have significant accounting and audit experience with ever-increasing responsibilities. I am particularly proud of leading my audit team to consistently completing our work ahead of target dates.

I have also been part of several successful client development efforts, and I found that to be both very rewarding and fun.

One of my career goals has been to work for a firm such as yours, and I am confident I can make a significant contribution from day one.

I am available for interview immediately. I will call you in several days to see if it is possible to arrange for a time for a personal interview.

Thank you for your attention.

Sincerely,

Jamal P. Wilson
166 Maple Lane, Ardmore PA 19005
(615) 123-4567 (Home) (615) 987-6543 (Cell)
jamalw44@gmail.com

Summary of Experience and Accomplishments – 17 years of progressive experience in management, maintenance, and training related to local and wide area networks, both PC and mainframes, and the applications associated with them. Extensive experience in the configuration and maintenance of Cisco routers and switches. Extensive experience in troubleshooting software and hardware problems and creating procedures and systems to avoid reoccurrence. Extensive experience in creating and managing large and complex databases.

Employment History –

XYZ College – Philadelphia, PA
July 2007–Present   **Networking & Network Security Instructor**
- Provide technical training and tutoring to college students.
- All courses student rated 8.5 or better on a 10-point scale.
- Courses include CCNA, Net+, A+, and Security+.
- Created training guides, chose textbooks.
- Canvassed local firms and created paid internships.
- Created online tutorials.
- Created and hosted local public TV show regarding computer security.

Major Tax Preparation Company – Media, PA
April 2006–July 2007   **Project Network Manager** (hired to execute a single project)
- Designed, installed, and configured Windows server network for a 20-office franchise in suburban Philadelphia—came in on time and under budget.
- Network features included Cisco VPN connectivity, Windows 7 desktops at each of 20 locations, full complement of servers, printers, and backup processes.

<u>Major National Bank</u> – Philadelphia, PA
March 2001–March 2006   **System Analyst**
- Total responsibility for maintaining and monitoring Cisco-based network operations for a worldwide network of ATMs, banking centers, and related financial transactions.
- Provided support for various legacy networks within the bank, including cross domains in the SNA environment, Stratacom, Nortel high-speed connectivity, and Racal.
- Member of 3-person project review team that had to sign off on any IT project work to be done throughout the company.
- Hired and supervised a 5-person onsite IT staff to ensure 24-7 reliability of systems and related applications.
- Prime interface with data and voice service providers; shopped suppliers every 2 years to ensure best possible pricing.

ABC Solutions Provider – Paoli, PA
July 1995–March 2001 **Network Engineer**
- Provided network customer support for a diverse customer base.
- Responsible for the design, installation, and configuration of wireless networking solutions.
- Responsible for maintaining full documentation for each assigned customer.
- Prime customer contact for upgrades and additional applications.

XYZ County Government – County Seat, PA
July 1991–June 1995   **Senior Systems Technician**
- Responsible for maintaining, troubleshooting, and repairing the county's data network and peripherals.

Education –
BA – Political Science, George Washington University, Washington, DC
Certificate in Information Technology – TEC, Rockville, MD

Jamal P. Wilson
166 Maple Lane, Ardmore PA 19005
(615) 123-4567 (Home) (615) 987-6543 (Cell)
jamalw44@gmail.com

Ms. Janice Philmont   Date
Director of Human Resources
Very Large IT Consulting Company
1930 Roosevelt Boulevard
Philadelphia, PA 19555

Dear Ms. Philmont:

I am a good friend of Bill Thompson, a network engineer in your Cleveland office. He advised me that an opening exists for a director of network operations in your Philadelphia office, a position for which he felt I was well qualified.

As can be seen by my enclosed resume, I have extensive experience in a wide variety of network operations, from design to maintenance, all including critical customer service aspects. I became known as a "go to" person with my peers; at Major National Bank, I was a member of the three-person project review team that had to sign off on all IT project work to be done by others anywhere within the company.

I have always wanted to do some teaching, so I took what has been a great job as an instructor at XYZ College, but after two years, it is time to get back where the IT action is. There is no better place to do that than with an IT consulting firm such as Very Large IT Consulting Company, where I can interface with a varied group of customers along with state-of-the-art technology and in a supervisory role help train others to do the same.

Thank you for considering my resume. I will follow up by phone to see if there is interest on your part.

Sincerely,

CHAPTER 8

Interviewing—
The Bridge Between You and Your Next Job!

The purpose of the interview process is to find out all there is to know about you to determine if you are the best person to hire from the pool of candidates being considered. Can you do the work, perform at a high level, and bring value to the organization? Are you a good fit for the "culture" of the organization and the people with whom you will be working?

Your job interviews will consist of two lines of questioning:

1.   Fact-finding questions to explore and determine your "hard" skills. Factual information; the what, when, how much, and for whom kind of information, such as the following:

   •   Do you have the required education, special training, any required certifications, and the like called for by the position to be filled?

   •   How does your work experience correlate to the job in question? How long will it take to get you "up and running"?

   •   How diversified is your pertinent work experience? Does your experience consist of a variety of tasks, responsibilities, and experiences, or have you done essentially the same activities over and over again? What is the depth of your experience?

   •   How knowledgeable are you regarding your general field (e.g., if in the accounting profession: GAAP, financial reporting standards, knowledge of the tax code, etc.)?

   •   How strong are your computer and software skills that correlate to the job and your general field of employment?

- How are your verbal skills? How are your persuasive skills?

- How are your writing skills? Has your experience shown that you are a skilled writer?

2. Behavioral questions to explore and determine your "soft" skills; seeking to understand what kind of a person you are and what makes you tick. Questions will begin with the following:

"Give me an example of …" or

"Tell me about a situation in which …" or

"Let me paint a picture and get your take on how you would address it."

The interviewer wants to learn such things as the following:

- How well do you get along with people?

- How have you handled interpersonal conflicts?

- Do you have a sense of humor?

- How do you think of yourself?

- How have you resolved problems big and small?

- How have you responded to deadlines?

- What leadership tendencies (if any) have you exhibited in the past?

- What are your interests outside of work?

The mission of the interviewer is to ask both fact finding and behavioral questions and then determine if you are a possible match for his or her organization and the job in question.

Typically, you will have multiple interviews with an organization before getting a job offer. In many cases, they will be with more than one person; expect multiple interviews with multiple interviewers.

Your mission is to make the cut each time; this is a "single elimination" process!

Some of this is determined through reference and background checks and perhaps testing, but much of it will come from the verbal back and forth of in-person interviews.

Before an offer can be extended, the interviewer and the organization need to *anticipate* what they will *know for sure* after you have been on the job for a few months.

You want to be sure that three things happen as a result of the verbal back and forth of these interviews.

1. *You answer all questions fully* to the satisfaction of the interviewer and, in doing so, paint the most favorable (but honest) portrait of yourself.

2. *You fill in the gaps* in the interviewer's battery of questions to make sure all of the positive and favorable aspects of you and your employment history are covered

3. *You don't raise red flags*; don't give the interviewer a reason to screen you out!

We will cover all three of these in great detail in this chapter.

The phone interview

Most likely the first interview you have will be a phone interview. The four components that follow apply just as much for a phone interview as for a face-to-face interview (preparation, etc.).

There are some aspects, however, that are unique to interviewing over the phone:

• You need a good phone. If using a cell phone, you need decent reception. If you get an incoming call asking for a phone interview and you are in a poor reception area, explain that to the caller and ask if you can call him or her back either from a landline or from another location.

- Ensure that there are no distractions—the dog is not barking, the TV is off, and so on.

- Focus, focus, focus. Focus on listening and your articulation. You don't want anything to get lost in the translation. If you have an accent, speak slowly, and enunciate carefully.

- Let your personality shine through. Show enthusiasm. You don't have the benefit of your personal appearance, so your voice has to carry the load. Smile as you talk on the phone; it will have an impact on your voice!

- Most probably the call will come from a contact you initiated. Using the retrieval system referred to in chapter 4, dig out your notes so you can talk of what you know about the firm, the challenges it faces, new products or services, and so on. You want to impress the interviewer that you know something about the firm other than the phone number and the fact that you are exploring seeking employment.

There are four distinct components of interviewing successfully:

1. **Preparation.** Anticipating every possible question that you will be asked, drafting a response to it, and rehearsing it. Preparing the questions you will ask.

2. **Getting your mental game together.**

3. **Making a great first impression ... Your opening approach.** You only get one chance for a first impression. How to begin the interview and get it right.

4. **Wrapping it up.** How to close out the interview and then how and when to follow up.

Let's explore each in detail.

1.   Preparation

You need to be prepared to answer any and every possible question you might be asked by an interviewer. You also need to be prepared to ask questions to flesh out full knowledge of both the job and of the organization. Later in this chapter, there is a list of standard questions you can expect to be asked as well as some sample questions you will be asking.

Write out the answers ... and rehearse

If you are going to do anything a multiple number of times, it makes great sense to figure out the very best way to do so and then "cookbook" the process as we discussed in chapter 3. Interviewing falls into this category.

You will be interviewed multiple times, often by different people at the same organization. You really need to nail the answers—every time. And the only way to do that is to draft—in writing—what you want to say as an answer. Then speak it aloud and then revise the answer to fit the spoken word. Ideally, have a friend or relative ask the questions, you speak out loud the answers in return, and have him or her critique your answers. You can read your answers for this exercise and then again edit the written responses. Is it time consuming? Yes. Is it worth it? Yes again!

The point is that you should never "wing it" answering a question. Your response needs to appear to be natural, an extension of your thought process. Yet you want to put the absolute correct spin on it—to convey the thoughts, ideas, and image putting you in the best possible light. And if you prepare properly, you should virtually *never* have to answer a question for the "first" time in an interview! You have answered it before in rehearsal and honed your answer to be the best possible answer.

Have you essentially memorized the meat of each answer? Yup, you sure have! To not do so is to risk not doing your best. Actors commit their lines to memory because they understand that without sticking 100% to the script, the story line will not be as clear and vivid as the producer and writers intended. Your interviews are no different.

It really isn't that hard. The process of modifying your answers and then rehearsing them will result in you remembering them.

Add "statements" to your answers when appropriate

As you draft your answers, take a tip from everyone that has been trained to give media interviews—use the question as a platform to both answer the question *and to make a statement.* An example is in order.

Question: Bill, tell me how you installed a new telephone and voice mail system on time and under budget as noted on your resume .

Answer: I began by creating a RFP based upon 95 percent of my budget and then gathered and analyzed the responses from seven vendors. I then asked for best and final proposals from three of those seven—the three with the best initial proposals. My RFP included a penalty for installation later than the target date and also a 3% bonus for being a week or more ahead of the target date with 100% functionality. Worked like a charm.

Statement: I learned the 95% of budget, late penalty, and early completion bonus concepts from my boss at XYZ Corp and have used them ever since. I have also modified them for staff incentives on projects. Everyone understands the objectives and what is at stake. As I said, it has worked for me every time.

So long as you answer the question and the statement is related to the question and answer—and not too long or elaborate—it will expand upon your answer to your benefit.

There are some things you *do not say* in any interview:

- Avoid anything derogatory or negative about past employers, past bosses, or those for whom you worked.

- Avoid exaggeration. Be specific about numbers.

- Avoid lengthy responses. You need to have a brief (but complete) response as well as an expanded answer for each question. The difference? Additional detail. Offer the brief answer, and if your interview says, "Tell me more," do so.

- Do not raise the subject of compensation or benefits. There is a time for that subject, and it is not for you to raise it except at the end of the interview if it hasn't been brought up by the interviewer.

- Avoid meandering responses. Answer the question. Be specific, be brief, and don't go wandering around the landscape. Don't be someone who upon being asked "What time is it?" proceeds to describe how to build a clock! Listen to the question, and answer it—specifically. Don't let a question about a past job in Philadelphia lead to an answer that includes a discussion about the Eagles football team or any similar digression. Your prospective employer wants to hire someone who can communicate effectively!

- Don't volunteer information that is not germane to the question. Here is an example:

  - Q: Tell me how you ended up here in Philadelphia when your previous job was in Florida.

  - A—Yes: The best opportunity was in Philadelphia, so I relocated.

  - A—No: The best opportunity was in Philadelphia, so I relocated. I really miss Florida, however, and someday want to get back there.

About truthfulness: always, always tell the truth

- Do not be guilty of lies of "commission"—puffing job titles, job descriptions, areas of responsibility, claiming a degree or professional accreditation you don't have or didn't earn.

- Do not be guilty of lies of "omission"—leaving out important information, not listing a job you had, fudging dates on your resume.

You *will* be found out, and everything else will come under suspicion. If you are found out before an offer is made, the offer usually won't be made. If you are found out after you are on the job, it would not be unheard of for you to be terminated.

Your references will be checked, unearthing discrepancies in degrees claimed, schools attended, job titles claimed, areas of responsibility claimed, and so on. Remember the examples of George O'Leary and Ronnie Few from the resume chapter!

Some commonly asked interview questions

1. "Tell me what you are looking for ... paint the picture for me," or "Tell me about yourself."

   This a question full of opportunities for you to screw up. Why? Because there can be a tendency to give a really bad answer! Really bad approaches and answers include the following:

a. **Touchy-feely.** Baring your soul about personal information—your children, your spouse, that you moved from Texas because of a divorce, how much you enjoy being a Cub Scout den leader, yada yada yada. An answer along these lines doesn't tell the interviewer a thing about why you are a good candidate for the job. I can't begin to count how many times over the years I have interviewed people and been subjected to what my children refer to as "TMI"—Too Much Information of a "who cares," unpleasant, or even embarrassing nature.

b. **I gotta get outta there.** If your motivation to be on the job market is to get away from an unfavorable situation (bad boss or bad organization), this is not the place to bring it up at all. Never, never, never bad-mouth a former boss or employer. If indeed you are leaving a job for reasons of incompatibility or a boss that you want to throttle, explain your decision in terms of seeking new challenges, that you are no longer learning, seeking an industry that is growing, and so on.

c. **I think this is what you want to hear.** Of course you pay attention to this. You are only going to say good things about yourself, but an experienced interviewer can easily spot a candidate that is trying to leave no possible good trait unmentioned.

What an interviewer wants to know in response to this question is this:

What is it about you that makes you a strong candidate for the job? What do you "bring to the table" that will make hiring you a good decision?

The opening statement

The correct way to answer this question is to have prepared an "opening statement". This opening statement is carefully prepared and well rehearsed. It will consist of "talking points"—concise statements of capability and achievement. Use them to answer this question, and if this question isn't asked, find a way to work in your opening statement in the first few minutes of the interview. If the first question is why you want to work there, say, "Well, first let me tell you a little about

95

myself," and go into your opening statement. Then answer the question that was asked.

Here is a sample opening statement:

- I appreciate the opportunity to meet with you and discuss how my background and achievements might be a good fit for the position of (position title) here at (name of organization).

- I am a graduate of (college or university) with a (degree granted) and have had an exciting and rewarding career in (field) thus far (only if your degree was granted less than ten years ago; skip this if it was more than ten years ago).

- I believe my record will indicate that I have strong people skills and an analytical approach to problem solving, and I am both a team player and a team builder. For example, the department I supervise recently moved into office space adjacent to another department in the company, and there was a real problem getting good interdepartmental cooperation. My team was frustrated by it, and making nice was not solving the problem. So I went to the other department head, who was also frustrated, and suggested that we institute two things:

  - First, I proposed a weekly pizza lunch meeting with both departments attending—a mandatory lunch meeting.

  - Second, at those meetings, each person had to address the group. One time it was to tell what they did and with whom they interacted. Another time, it was to tell the group something about them that the other group members would not know if they hadn't been told. For example, I told them that I played the trombone in my high school band.

  - Within a month, we had peace and harmony between the two departments. I am really proud of that accomplishment.

- I have been fortunate to have had a chance to make presentations on behalf of my current employer, be on the new client orientation team, and otherwise contribute to the growth of the firm.

- I would not be looking to make a change were it not for the fact that my mom is in her late eighties and failing, so I moved here to Houston to be able to assist her far better than I could when I was a two-hour flight away.

- I am easily adaptable to change and eager to make a real contribution wherever I end up.

- Does that sort of paint the picture for you?

The total time to recite this is about two minutes. Draft your one or two concrete examples of what you accomplished—what happened because you were there and made it happen. They become the specific selling points for your candidacy when answering this question. You want to indicate the kind of value contribution you will bring to your new position if hired.

Finally, about your opening statement: be brief, be specific, be focused, and don't ramble (but why would you—you rehearsed it, right?).

2. "What do you know about our industry and our company?"

- Research of the organization and of the interviewer beforehand is a must as discussed previously. Check LinkedIn and do a Google search on his or her name. Not doing this research is inexcusable and will hurt you during the interview and consideration process. It tells the interviewer that the interview wasn't important enough to gather this information!

- Know the company's sales and current issues. Check for press releases on the company website or by a search. Do some basic research on the industry and see if you can determine who the firm's prime competitors are.

- And when answering this question, pull from your portfolio information about the organization taken from their website and make reference to it. Your interviewer can't help but be impressed!

3. "What is your understanding of the job?"

- If you know it, play it back. If you only know part of it, say, "I'm not totally sure of the details, but as I understand it, it is (verbalize what you do know)."

4. "What do you do for fun?"

- Be careful here. If you like to dress up as a clown and then go to sports bars to drink, this is *not* the time to mention it!

- Talk of your more "normal" things, such as biking, reading, and so on.

5. "What do you look for in a job?"

- Talk of "growth," "challenge," and a chance to make "a contribution."

- Do *not* talk of benefits and promotion opportunities!

6. "What would you 'bring to the table' here at XYZ?"

- Talk of past contributions and experience and how they might fit in.

7. "What is it that you will bring that makes you the person to hire?"

- Use the talking points in your opening statement to talk of previous accomplishments and so on.

8. "What do you do to stay healthy?"

- Don't exaggerate. If you say, "I run half marathons," it best be true! The interviewer may say, "Me too, and the company sponsors one, so I will look forward to you being part of that!"

9. "If I were to ask your last boss the areas where improvement would have increased your contributions, what would he or she say?" or "What are your weaknesses?"

- Saying that you have none is not the way to go here.

- Do some self-analysis to answer this question, and talk of the areas that were discussed in your performance reviews. Do so in a nondefensive manner. Try to tie in your answer to the type of job you are applying for. For example, if applying for a staff accountant position, reply that "I guess I am a bit of a perfectionist, which is great at work, but it sometimes drives my friends crazy."

- If possible, talk of a weakness that resulted in a learning episode. "I tend to be a bit of a perfectionist, and in the past, it has resulted in taking too much time to do a task. Double- and triple-checking takes time. I have really worked on this, and while I am very much into error-free work, I have leaned to check it once and move on, and that has increased my output."

- Be sure to cover the major areas that will come up in reference checks with former bosses, as your references will be checked, and you don't want that former boss to raise issues that you didn't! This is also a double-check of "know you own flaws and weaknesses." It shows that you know of them and are working to improve in those areas.

10. "Likewise, if I were to ask your last boss the areas where you excelled, what would he or she say?"

    - Stress your accomplishments here.

11. "Tell me about your last boss."

    - Talk of positives. Everyone has them, so talk of them.

    - Do not talk of problems or difficulties unless you think they will come up in a reference check and unless it is the reason you are making a voluntary change. If you do address them, make the issues factual rather than opinion.

12. "What annoys you?"

    - Make them business oriented, such as people who procrastinate, people making the same mistake twice, and so on.

    - Don't stray from business-related topics, such as slow drivers, being stuck in traffic, and so on.

13. "Tell me of an interpersonal conflict at work and how you handled it."

    - Be sure to tell the cause of the conflict—the nature of it—and then what you did to resolve it successfully.

14. "What prompted your move from (area) to here?"

    - Talk of opportunity and flexibility.

15. "What was the last book you read?"

    - Be prepared to not only answer the question but then to respond to the possible follow-up questions of "What was it about? What did you get out of it?"

    - Just as with the question about what you like to do for fun, be careful. If you like to read "how to build a bomb at home" books or romance novels, this is *not* the place to bring it up! Hopefully, you (also) read books of real content, regardless of their genre.

16. "Tell me about a mistake you made."

    - Think this one through before determining your answer. You want the response to be reflective of a learning episode.

    - And you have certainly made mistakes!

17. "If someone didn't like you, what reason would he or she give?"

    - Again, think this one through. You know there are those that don't care for you. There has to be. Give an answer that is still positive. "Some people don't like that I am pretty assertive in getting things done. I guess I have run over some people that I felt didn't move fast enough."

Answering the tough questions

18. "Why have you had so many jobs in the past five years?"

    - To the extent possible, point out that former employers relocated, closed, went out of business, and so on—all good reasons to change jobs. For the others, have a reasonable explanation as to why you made a job change, based upon opportunity, a negative change in the job after you were on board for a while, a boss who didn't help you learn, and so on.

19. "Were you fired (from the job at XYZ)?"

- If the answer is yes, then say so and explain, casting the circumstances in the best possible yet accurate light.

20. When the job you are applying for is a "promotion" step up: "What makes you think you are ready to become a (manager, controller, etc.)?" Consider any of the following responses:

- I have thought about this carefully. With a thorough understanding and the mission of the job, I know I can be successful … and can hit the ground running.

- I have done many of the functions associated with this job in the past. Let me elaborate (and then do so).

21. "What salary are you looking for?"

- Answer carefully. Hopefully you know the salary range ahead of time. If so, you answer, "I know the salary range is $X to $Y. My last salary and bonus plan paid $Z on an annual basis. While I feel my experience qualifies me to be at the high end of your range, I am primarily looking for opportunity first and am prepared to be flexible about the compensation package."

- If you don't know the range, then you answer, "Well, my last salary and bonus plan paid $Z on an annual basis. While I would prefer to make some upward strides, I am primarily looking for opportunity first and am prepared to be flexible about the compensation package." Never inflate your current or past compensation. It is not uncommon for an employer to ask to see a W-2, and you are sunk if it doesn't match what you have said.

- By these responses, you have put a salary number on the table.

If for some reason you aren't asked this question, toward the end of the interview, say, "We haven't discussed compensation. What is the range?" And from there, offer the first response above.

Questions you will ask

You need to be just as prepared to ask questions as to answer them. In this case, however, you can have them in written form and refer to them and jot responses if you wish.

The following are "must ask" questions; they are designed to achieve two objectives:

• Gather information so you know as much as possible about the organization and the job (if asked, you should be able to not only describe the job but also to answer questions about it and the organization).

• Further sell yourself to the interviewer.

When the interviewer asks if you have any questions, you respond, "Yes, I do." Then proceed to ask those that have not been addressed thus far, such as the following:

1. Why do you like working here?

2. How would you describe the atmosphere, culture, or environment here?

3. Why is the position open?

4. How successful was the person that was in this job before it became open?

5. What are most important factors to succeed in this position?

6. What are most important factors to succeed here at XYZ?

7. What are the plans for the future for XYZ? Growth? Expansion?

8. What is the structure of the job and the department?

9. What is the next step after our interview? How soon might I hear back?

And ask follow-up questions as necessary to flesh out a full understanding of the answers provided.

Finally, not unlike the advice given to a witness in a trial, be cautious as to what you "volunteer." Stick to your prepared answers.

Remember that one of your objectives is to *not* raise any red flags!

As you interview, keep in mind the dynamics facing interviewers and the organizations for whom they work. It is not the hiring of people that gives HR people and CEOs nightmares. It is the "unhiring" of people that does!

A bad hire that leads to a termination is—at best—troublesome. It will negatively impact coworkers and perhaps customers. In our litigious society, a bad hire that results in a contested termination can become a disastrous nightmare—lawsuits, huge settlements, tarnished reputations ... and the list goes on.

Is it any wonder, therefore, that one of the basic objectives of interviewers is to screen out potential problem candidates? Yes, their mission is to sell the job and sell the organization to each person they interview, but they also don't want anyone to slip through the screening process that can become a problem employee and trigger the need to terminate.

That is why you need to be primed to commit no errors that raise red flags. You must demonstrate that you do not have a "chip on your shoulder" and, furthermore, that you are not the kind of person to have one. You don't want to exhibit those personality characteristics and background history aspects that say, "This person could become a problem."

You need to demonstrate beyond a doubt that you have a teamwork attitude, that you are adaptable to change, that you speak kindly of all.

And if you indeed do have some of these "unfavorable" characteristics, here is the perfect opportunity to truly work to make some changes within yourself.

If you are unemployed—and have been for some time—or if you have recently been let go, you may well have gained a perspective that prepares you to make some changes within yourself. You may have well experienced what is often referred to as a "SEE"—Significant Emotional Event.

A SEE is an event that shakes people to the core, forcing them to reexamine themselves in the cold light of day to determine why what happened to them in fact happened. A SEE may help you address the things that can have an impact on making the cut during the interview process such as the following:

- Watch your attitude—you must display a positive one. Ask those who know you to tell you true, do you sometimes demonstrate a negative attitude? If so, work on it.

- You want to be seen as friendly, warm, and congenial. Be sure you pass the "Tulsa Test" (would a total stranger enjoy sitting next to you on a long-distance flight to Tulsa?).

- You want to project that you are a rational, logical, and adaptable person and that you understand that the real world is not perfect.

- If you have ever cited an employer (filed an action against an employer), bring it up, and explain it thoroughly. If it was discharged as without merit, you have a problem. Sorry about that, but you carry a red flag the size of a blanket on your back. The best you can do is to explain the circumstances and make your case logically.

Be yourself, but also project a person that is likeable, realistic, enthusiastic, and not argumentative.

Interviewers are people too—how to avoid annoying your interviewer!

Let's take a look at your interviewer. We have reviewed his or her motives—to find out all about you and not to let future problem employees slip through the cracks. What else?

What bugs you? Gum crackers, loud talkers, or mumblers? Well, guess what? Those same things also annoy interviewers. Wouldn't it be nice to know the likes and dislikes of the interviewer across the desk from you? Well, you can. Just think it through. They are very logical and a function of both human nature and the interviewer's job.

Remember, the interviewer has two tasks:

1. The first is to screen against the criteria for the job, screen for "hard" skills and experience (what have you done, and how well did you do it) as well as "soft" skills (personality, interpersonal communications, and the like). Don't underestimate the impor-

tance of strong "soft" skills. *Remember, more people get jobs, lose jobs, get promoted, and get fired for poor communications and people skills than any other single reason!* During the interview, it is your communications skills that are being probed; your resume *should* tell much of what you did and how well you did it!

2. The interviewer's other job is to always sell the organization (generate great PR for the organization) and to sell the job if you pass the muster. If you don't pass the muster, his or her job is to then let you down easy.

Regardless, they are human, and you need to eliminate from your person those things that are turnoffs—those habits that will annoy the interviewers and distract them from liking you as a person. So read on and pay attention:

• Focus, focus, focus. A lack of focus on your part (not tying your answers together, not giving sufficiently specific answers, wandering around the verbal landscape) can hurt you big time! Not asking follow-up or clarifying questions and tying in your comments to the organization and its industry doesn't help your cause. You have rehearsed every possible question you might be asked, so tie together your answers into a coherent story. Use the questions as a platform to tell your story while still answering the question.

• Remember, you are on someone else's turf. If the interviewer is behind a desk, don't put anything on the desk, and don't rearrange anything on it. Keep your hands, notebook, and other items on your lap. The desk is the interviewer's territory!

• Do not display an over-abundance of enthusiasm. Enthusiasm is good—but in moderate doses. Have enthusiasm, but do not come across as a "warm Coca-Cola fizzing over." Don't end an answer with a great big smile like the cat that ate the canary. Don't be like the candidate I once interviewed that, at the conclusion of every statement, sat up straight and gave me a smile that was unnerving … like a puppy waiting for a biscuit.

• Be on time. The interviewer has a schedule. When you are late, two things happen. Your interviewer falls behind schedule, and you have communicated that being on time is not one of your strong suits. Both are not good.

- Balance the talking with the listening. Listen to what one recruiter/interviewer had to say: "People who ramble on and on and never shut up drive me up a wall. I once interviewed a candidate where I asked one question, and ten minutes later, she was still talking. She rambled around the landscape verbally. I tried to break in. Finally, I said loudly, 'Enough.' She looked at me with a startled look!"

- Know when there is too little versus too much conversation. Interviewers will ask open-ended questions. You know that. You know that your job is to answer them succinctly and to the point (as rehearsed!). Do not be too wordy—see above. Think of it this way: you have a fifty-cent answer and a one-dollar answer to every question you might be asked. The difference is the degree of detail. When you offer up the fifty-cent answer and the interview either says, "Tell me more," or just nods expectantly, add the other fifty cents of details. Don't make an interviewer "pull teeth" to get information from you.

- Make eye contact! You don't want to stare, and you don't want to look like a bug-eyed madman or serial killer. You also don't want to *never* make eye contact. And there is such a thing as "warm" eye contact and "scary" eye contact. You are not trying to pull a "Dirty Harry" look on the interviewers, just an acknowledgment that they are whom you are talking to. You can smile with your eyes, eyebrows raised, showing rapport and interest.

- Be conscious of smell and scents. It's an interview, not a date or a night on the town. Ladies, use just a slight touch of your favorite fragrance. The operative term is "slight." Men, aftershave is fine. Skip the cologne; it is much stronger. No one wants to think they walked into a florist shop as a result of *your* fragrance. And do we need to remind you to dump the gum before you walk into the building? I didn't think so.

- No dark glasses, no tinted glasses, and no cell phone earpiece.

- Avoid the "I work here" look. You can't overdress for an interview if you rule out the tux and evening gown. Ever hear the phrase "first impressions ..."? Of course you have. So dress like it. Don't insult the interviewer and the organization by dressing like you didn't remember that this was a job interview.

Men, wear a suit, a conservative tie, long-sleeved dress shirt (never short sleeved!). Polished shoes and minimal jewelry complete the ensemble. Lose the earring if you have one.

Women, wear a pants suit or business skirt suit, minimal jewelry, and no necklines that are more appropriate for a Saturday night. Wear shoes that are businesslike.

And for both genders, if it is cold, wear an overcoat or trench coat, not your ski jacket over your suit. That looks tacky.

This is a time for self-evaluation. Ask your spouse or best friend for his or her advice about those things that—because he or she loves you—he or she lets slide by. Tell him or her that you are on a self-improvement kick and *really* want to know what you do that could well annoy your interviewer!

Observe these simple guidelines, and you will go a long way to avoiding the interviewers "pet peeves."

2.   Getting your mental game together

A very subtle—yet important—aspect of a successful interview is to have your mental game in order.

Having your mental game together means the following:

- You have the mental confidence that comes from being 100% prepared to interview. You have memorized and rehearsed every answer to virtually any question that comes your way. You have researched the organization and the interviewer to the extent that information is available; you have some pertinent facts about the interviewer in your notes. You have the questions you will ask in your notes. You have your opening statement ready and memorized. And when we say memorized, we don't necessarily mean every single word but certainly every talking point and the right words to express it.

- As you walk into the building where your interview will take place, you are mentally rehearsing your opening statement.

- You have gotten a good night's rest and are refreshed with great energy.

- Your mental attitude reflects how you feel about your appearance. You want to look like a million bucks. Business attire all the way.

- You have cleared your mind of any possible distractions. Don't think about what you need to do later in the day. You can't appear to be distracted and still have a successful interview.

- You are going to be suitably assertive. You will look the interviewer in the eye (but not in a menacing manner); you will sit up straight and even lean forward when speaking. You will listen carefully and not interrupt. You will take notes.

- You will smile when appropriate, and when the interviewer speaks, listen carefully and nod your head in agreement—it demonstrates that you are paying attention and understand what is being said. At all costs, avoid daydreaming, looking around the room, and so on.

- You have mentally edited your behavior to eliminate all annoying mannerisms. No jingling of change in the pockets and no ear tugging or knuckle cracking. Ask those that know you well what annoying mannerisms you have, and then purge them from your person. It wasn't until a close friend told me that I slouched that I realized it, and now I focus on walking and standing straight and tall. How about you? Ask! Then have a mental checklist of what not to do, a "mantra," if you will.

- For you younger types – refrain from using the lingo and slang terms that only you and your generation use or understand. No prefacing a sentence with "like" and using any other similar term that your interviewer's children will understand better than the interviewer!

- You know where you are going, and you will arrive early. Nothing can ruin your mental game faster than being late. If in doubt, do a dry run the day before. Remember – five minutes early is "on time"!

- You have several extra copies of your resume along with your notes for this interview in a nice leather or leatherette portfolio, not a mangled and soiled manila folder.

- You have a nice quality pen to take notes, one without advertising on it. It doesn't have to expensive. A five- or six-dollar pen from an office supply chain will do.

- You have your calendar for the next few weeks with you. You don't want to say, "I'll have to get back to you," if the interviewer suggests a date for a follow-up interview.

3. Making a great first impression ... Your opening approach

You want the first impression you make on everyone you meet in life to be totally favorable. I suggest you work on this for all of your waking life. I have. Smile at gas station and convenience store clerks—people you may never see again. Say, "Have a nice day," to others in the elevator. Hold doors open for the folks behind you. Why? Well, first of all, why not? But selfishly, it puts you in a mode to be a person who is "nice," "kind," and "friendly." There is nothing wrong with that! And when you walk into a job interview (or to see your prospective in-laws for the first time!), it will then be second nature to send off the vibe "I am a nice, kind, and caring person." It has to be sincere; just be a regular and nice person, and the sincerity will come through!

Nowhere is a great first impression more important than in the job-seeking process.

It doesn't begin with the interviewer. It begins with the very first person you meet at the interview location. It might be a security guard in the building lobby, or it may be the receptionist or administrative assistant that greets you as you arrive at the actual interview location. You will never know who has whose ear, but you can be assured that many times his or her opinion of you will be asked. The question is, what will this person say? So be on your very most charming behavior.

Making a great first impression includes these things:

- Give a big smile—not phony, but sincere—and not just initially. Keep a series of facial expressions on your face that are smile based. No, you don't want to grin all the time, but don't be somber either.

- Walk with confidence, but do not strut.

- Have a great appearance. Wear conservative business attire all the way. Good grooming means clothes pressed, shoes not scuffed, nails groomed, hair in place, very little if any fragrance to distract. You don't have to be dressed in the height of fashion, but make sure your wardrobe isn't dated. The same goes for eyeglasses, hairstyle, and so on. Wear no more than one ring to a hand, one bracelet to a wrist, and one earring to an ear.

- Ensure that your cell phone is silenced.

- Greet everyone "Good morning" or "Good afternoon."

- State your purpose until you get to the actual interviewer: "I am here to meet with Mr. Roger Johnson. I have a 3:00 o'clock appointment. My name is Harry Smith."

- While you sit in a reception area, be aware you are probably being observed, perhaps by the interviewer's personal administrative assistant. Do not make cell calls, and do not text; read whatever is in the reception area or review your notes about the organization. Sit still; don't wander about. Don't groom yourself in the reception area; the time and place to do that is before you get there.

Time to begin the interview ... your opening approach

- Offer a firm but not bone-crushing handshake; no "dead fish" grip either. Practice it if you are in doubt.

- Give a big smile.

- Introduce yourself, "Hello, Mr. Johnson. I'm Katie Harris. Thank you for seeing me today."

- Always refer to the interviewer as "Mr." or "Ms." unless they tell you otherwise.

- Rather than wait for the interviewer to start talking, as soon as you are in the interviewer's office, say, "I am really looking forward to talking with you about this position and XYZ. I have done some research regarding XYZ, and I am most interested."

And then, take it from there. Here are some hints:

- Don't take a beverage into the interview if you had one in the reception area. There is probably no good place to put it, and you don't want to run the risk of a spill.

- Have a notepad in your lap, and jot down notes as appropriate. Your questions are also there for you to refer to.

- Sit up straight, don't slouch, and don't fidget.

- If the interviewer is very informal, you should still maintain a businesslike approach. Do not be too stiff, just warm and businesslike.

- Keep good eye contact with the interviewer.

4.   Wrapping it up - closing out the interview ... and follow-up

The interview is coming to an end. You have a statement to make and one more question to ask.

Even if the job sounds like it is not what you are looking for, you don't want to take yourself out of the running at this point in time. Why? Because unless it is so far off the mark to leave no doubt, you need to think it through, compare it to other jobs you are exploring, and see how it unfolds. And it is not uncommon for the actual job offer to be different—to a greater or lesser degree—than the job you were originally interviewing for. This is due to the interviewer realizing the depth and breadth of your experience and background and then realizing where you might better make a contribution to his or her organization. Sometimes this is in another already-defined job and sometimes in a job to be modified to take advantage of your credentials.

So back to the statement and question you need to ask.

The statement: "Mr. Johnson, I have really enjoyed talking with you, and I must tell you that I am most interested in exploring becoming part of the XYZ team."

The question: "Mr. Johnson, what is the next step in this process? When might I expect to hear from you regarding my candidacy?"

Take note of the answer. If another interview is scheduled, be sure to note the time and date and ask, "Who might I be talking to at that time?"

Take your leave, offer a firm handshake, and say, "Thank you again for meeting with me."

Later that day, send an e-mail to the interviewer, restating, "Mr. Johnson, I really enjoyed talking with you today, and I must tell you that I am most interested in exploring becoming part of the XYZ team."

Make sure your notes are in order, and then move on to waiting and other interviews!

Summary

- Understand that the job of the interviewer is to gather information and *screen out* potential problem employees.

- Do not raise any red flags!

- Preparation is critical to a successful interview:

- Write answers to every question you anticipate you will be asked, and then rehearse them so they have virtually been memorized. Draft your answers carefully.

- Prepare a strong "opening statement"; know it cold.

- Be prepared to add "statements" to your answers where appropriate.

- Prepare the questions you will ask the interviewer.

- Rehearse, rehearse, rehearse.

- Know what annoys most people, and work to avoid these mannerisms and characteristics.

- Get your mental game together; be mentally prepared to interview.

- Plan your opening approach; be sure you make a great first impression.

- Take good notes.

- Have a plan to close out the interview and determine the next step.

CHAPTER 9

Job-Seeking Strategy—Uncovering the Hidden and Unpublished Job Market

What is the "hidden and unpublished job market"?

The term "hidden job market" refers to job openings that exist or will in the very near future but that are not available to the general job-seeking public; they are not being advertised, are not on the Internet job boards, and are not listed with staffing services. They may or may not be listed on the employer's website.

What are they then? How can an employer hope to fill a job opening that no one else knows about?

The need for the "hidden" aspect has several reasons:

- The job is currently filled by an incumbent who is going to be terminated in the near term for performance-related reasons, but the employer wants to control the timing of the termination, hence the need to keep under wraps the fact that a job opening will exist soon.

- The job is currently filled by an incumbent who has given notice of intent to resign in the near future, but the employer and incumbent want to control the timing of the announcement and resignation, hence the need to keep under wraps the fact that a job opening will exist soon.

- The job is currently filled by an incumbent who is going to be either terminated or reassigned to another job in the near term as part of a reorganization, but the employer wants to control the timing of the announcement of the reorganization, hence the need to keep under wraps the fact that a job opening will exist soon.

- The job does not yet exist. The employer is waiting for the completion of a pending event—the awarding of a contract, finalization of an acquisition, some definitive result that will require additional people—but the employer will not begin the hiring process until the need is firm.

A factor about these jobs that is particularly attractive is that until they actually surface, there is little or no "competition" for you to contend with! If you can get your credentials in front of a decision maker with one of these jobs to fill, you have a definite leg up on any other outside candidates.

So how do you get your foot in the door for these "hidden" jobs?

- **Timing.** Due to the nature of most of the hidden jobs, timing is critical, which means you need to be ready at a moment's notice to respond. LinkedIn and Facebook profiles have to be current and in good shape. Resume and cover letter both need to be up to date and ready to send. Interview question responses need to be completed and ready to be reviewed in the event that a telephone interview is in the cards very quickly after initiating action.

- **Check your sources frequently**, perhaps every day—job boards, prearranged searches of target organizations using the "site:" field command discussed in chapter 5, websites of targeted employers with available job listings, classified ads, and so on. When a hidden job becomes "unhidden," you want to know about it and be ready to act that day, not a week later. Ben Franklin had it right when he talked of early birds and worms!

- **Networking.** As noted in the title of the great networking book by Harvey Mackay, *Dig Your Well Before You're Thirsty*, you build your network before you need it. If your network is skimpy, however, use what you have, and get to work to build it to a far more robust level. We will cover how to put your existing network to work for you to unearth the hidden job market, but you should make building your network a priority. My advice to you is to buy—and read—Harvey's book!

If you can't give yourself an "A" in networking, get started on it today. Although current efforts to build your network may not help much for a current job search, there will be great value in the future of having a strong and diverse network. Just as the Internet has made basic research much, much easier, it has had a similar impact on networking. LinkedIn and Facebook—to name just two—of the networking websites offer a great chance to build your network and stay in touch with many. Adding people to your network is easy; staying in contact with them is not. Making phone calls is one way, but caution is offered. Unless you have a strong relationship with someone, avoid "howdy" calls—they simply waste both your time and that of the person called. A "howdy" call is just that. "How are you? ... I am fine ... yada yada yada." This kind of reminds me of the sign hanging in my cousin Martin's office: "Never Try to Teach a Pig to Dance—It Wastes Your Time and Annoys the Pig!" The same principle applies to making "howdy" calls.

Sending e-mails and snail mail with clippings and articles of interest is an excellent way to stay in touch with people. Announcements regarding your organization might make the list of things to send of value. Ever since I have been in the business world, I have sent a holiday card in mid-December with a short personal note and include a family photo. I get comments every year from people I talk with and see infrequently but who enjoy getting my card and family photo. My list is a long one—some 250 names—and a great way for me to stay in touch. I don't really care if I get a card back. My purpose is to reach out and stay in touch!

Create an e-mail distribution list, and use it to forward articles of interest and the like that you have come across. Just be careful to not become a pest. Once a month or every three weeks is fine. Once a week is overload. And make sure it is of value to the recipients.

There are many great books—including Harvey Mackay's—and resources on networking available, so we won't go into more detail here, but make building your network a regular entry on your daily to-do list.

- **Have and execute a self-marketing plan.** This is the most proactive way to unearth those hidden jobs—as well as those that are not hidden but you have just not found yet.

Self-marketing plan

This self-marketing plan involves you making lots of phone calls and following a carefully worded script (see notes accompanying each aspect of the call):

"Bill. Harry Smith here. How have you been? It has been a while since we talked."

Hopefully it will not have been so long that Bill hasn't a clue who you are! Networks and contacts are like tuna salad—the fresher the better. If it has been awhile or the person is just a business card you collected at a meeting a year ago, you should add this:

"Bill, you may not remember, but we met at the XYZ meeting/conference/reception/whatever last year in (city). I enjoyed our brief conversation then, and I was impressed. I kept your business card, knowing that I would want to touch base with you in the future—like now when I need some advice!

"Say, Bill, I have a favor to ask. Nothing heavy, mind you, but important to me. I am in the process of changing jobs, and I really need a critical eye to take a look at my resume. I respect your judgment and know I can count on you to tell me like it is."

Note what you have done. First, you have paid Bill a compliment. We all like getting a compliment. Second, you did not ask Bill for a job or if he had an opening. You never want to ask that question. It puts people on the spot, makes them uncomfortable, and puts them in a position to usually say no—and people don't like to do that, especially to a friend or acquaintance.

"May I e-mail my resume to you and then get some feedback in a few days?"

You asked Bill to do something that is both very easy and will take very little time, so virtually all asked will say yes.

"Great! I will also include my target list of possible employers, and it would be most helpful if you knew anyone at those firms. Getting my resume in front of a decision maker is my objective. I can get that feedback at the same time I get your read on my resume."

Bill has already said yes once; he is not going to say no to this add-on request, although it is a bit more time consuming. The target list has been compiled through your knowledge of the area's finest employers, newspaper articles regarding those firms that are expanding, and those firms posting jobs that are of interest. Limit listings to one page only of fifteen to twenty companies.

"Bill, I can't thank you enough. I really appreciate your input. I am working on my schedule, and I need to be near your office in the next few days. Can I swing by your office and take a few minutes of your time to get your feedback? What day and time will work for you. I am at your disposal."

How well Bill knows you will determine how successful you are in getting a personal meeting. If you can hit 50% on these, you are doing great. Why do you want a personal meeting rather than a telephone conversation? You will have Bill's full and uninterrupted attention and an opportunity to impress Bill with your demeanor and personality. Refresh Bill's memory of how sharp and personable you are. All of this is harder to do over the phone.

If Bill can't grant a personal meeting, say this:

"Hey, no problem. I will give you a call in a few days or so to get your feedback. Thanks again. You will have my resume and target list within the hour. Let me confirm your e-mail address."

You want an agreement that Bill will take your call and give you the input you want on your resume as well as the details regarding who Bill knows on your target list. You have also confirmed Bill's e-mail address. Send him your resume and your target list as e-mail attachments (done in MS Word, of course) along with the following e-mail:

Bill,

Thanks so much for taking my call today. I am excited about the challenges of a new position, and I really appreciate your candid review of my resume Does it flow? Is it clear as to my achievements? Any and all comments will be appreciated. I have also attached a target list of employers I am interested in, and it would be most helpful if you have any contacts at any of them that can get me past the gatekeepers in HR.

And of course, let me know who else you think I should be talking to.

Thanks again, and I will give you a call in a few days.

Regards,

Harry Smith

The operative words in this e-mail are "resume review" and "who do you know." In order to review your resume, Bill has to read it. First mission accomplished—you have a potential employer (depending on where Bill is located and what his business is) reading your resume, and you have a "sphere of influence" reading your resume.

What is a "sphere of influence"? They are people whose positions and achievements make them valuable contacts in and of themselves *and* because of who they know and who is in their networks.

People talk with people of all walks of life but particularly with peers. Spheres of influence talk to other spheres of influence. You make this kind of call to enough spheres of influence, and sooner or later, you are going to hit one who either has a job opening—hidden or not—and/or knows someone who is in a hiring mode.

But Bill's job is not to find you a job. Bill is busy (or else he wouldn't be a good sphere of influence!). You need to follow up! If you can get the personal face time with Bill, great. If not, make this call three to four days after you e-mailed your information to Bill:

"Bill—Harry Smith here. Is this a good time to talk?

(If you have a hard time connecting with Bill, e-mail him and request a time to make the call.)

"Just following up on our recent conversation and the e-mail I sent you. What are your thoughts on my resume?"

At this point, don't talk anymore. You want, gently, to make Bill talk to you about your resume. Depending on how certain you are regarding the content of your resume, you really want Bill's comments. Listen intently, make notes, and recognize that he may have some good input to fine-tune your resume. If you get a blanket "looks good," ask a few questions such as these:

"Bill, if you were to make one recommendation to improve my resume, what would it be?"

"Does it flow smoothly, or are there are areas that are confusing?"

Do not be defensive or argumentative about any comments Bill makes!

"Thanks. That was really helpful.

"As to my target list, let's see There are about twenty firms listed on it. Do you have any contacts at any of those I can leverage to see if they have an opportunity where I can make a contribution?"

Make sure your list is no longer than fifteen to twenty firms. Any more than one sheet of paper becomes an imposition. If Bill says, "Yes, I do at XYZ," ask for the information.

Where does this target list come from? Think carefully about some basic criteria: what industries are you interested in and seem capable of weathering whatever the future may hold for them; what industries and jobs seem to be trending upward in growth, popularity, and stability; location based upon your commute, including public transportation; locations where you would be willing to move (a local move) or relocate (move to a different city or state). As a result of this thinking and study, prepare a target list of fifteen to twenty companies, nonprofits, government agencies, and other employers. This is your target list. In addition to whatever job opportunities come your way, you want to find a way to get your credentials in front of a decision maker at each organization on your target list.

Back to your request of Bill. If Bill offers to make a call on your behalf, you have a decision to make.

If Bill is not a close friend, decline his offer by saying this:

"Bill, I appreciate the offer, but let me make the call, mentioning that you referred me. It will help me get a feel for the organization. I will let you know how the call goes, and I may ask you to make a follow up call or e-mail."

Why don't you want Bill to make the call? Because you can never be sure that he did make the call! It is not a priority for Bill, it can fall by the wayside, and you sure can't call him back to ask him if he made the call!

On the other hand, if you and he are very, very close and *you have no doubt* he will make the call, then you will say this:

"Great. Who will you be calling so I can follow up a few days after your call? How about if I make the follow-up call in a week?

"One last question, Bill. Can you think of any other people or organizations I need to contact? Is there someplace I have overlooked that comes to mind?"

This is one last effort to get any additional leads from Bill.

"Okay, Bill, I really appreciate your help. It has been most valuable. Thanks again, and I will keep you posted as to my progress. If something comes to mind, just give me a shout or send me an e-mail. It would be greatly appreciated."

Is this whole process a bit assertive? Yes, it is – and it is understandable that you might not be comfortable making these calls at first. Keep in mind two things – first, virtually all of the people you call won't think poorly of you for making the call. Second – it works and is a viable strategy for you to find a new job. So gut up and make the calls!

To whom do you make these calls?

Everyone! Yes, everyone you can think of!

You are going to make calls to your network of contacts with some modifications, depending on who you are calling.

When calling business associates, follow the menu above 100%.

How about others to call other than business associates? Think of it this way: the person that sat in your dentist's chair before you may well have bemoaned to your dentist the fact that he or she is having a tough time finding someone for a critical job—same for your doctor, and same for your priest, minister, rabbi, and so on.

You want to modify the opening resume request slightly to this:

"Frank. Harry Smith here. How have you been? It has been a while since we talked."

Depending on the frequency of contact with each person, you may need to remind him or her of who you are and how you are connected to one another. If necessary, do so as was covered before with the "Bill" example.

"Say, Frank, I have a favor to ask. Nothing heavy, mind you, but important to me. I am in the process of changing jobs and trying to make sure I leave no stone unturned looking for opportunities.

"I would really appreciate it if I could e-mail you my resume so you can see my work history and then give some thought as to who I should be talking to. I will also send you my target list of firms I am most interested in, and it would be great if you knew someone at any of them. Will you do that for me?

"What is your e-mail address?"

And take it from there!

There might be some contacts where it is better to e-mail your request with your resume and target list as attachments. For those that do not work with a telephone at hand, such as your doctor and dentist, this is a better approach. When you call and want to talk to those types of professionals, you are taking them away from their primary work. Better to let them hear your request on their downtime.

A job created just for you?

A side benefit of this self-marketing effort is that sometimes a job gets created just for you! This can happen in two different ways:

• Almost every department has an individual who is underperforming to a greater or lesser degree. To the extent that the department head—or his or her boss—has bigger issues to worry about, that underperforming worker's job is safe. But sooner or later, that worker will be terminated, the objective being to replace him or her with a worker who can perform at a higher level. Oftentimes, the trigger point is to have in hand the resume of that potential replacement—namely, you! Upon seeing your credentials, the lightbulb goes on in the mind of a decision maker that "here is the replacement for Harry who is just not cutting it in the accounting department!"

- The company can't afford to not hire this talented person. Good managers know that sometimes they come across a person so good that it makes good business sense to use his or her talents to assist the department or organization achieve its goals. This is done in one of two ways:

  - To do some reorganizing of existing staff to reallocate existing talent and merge into the lineup the "new talent"—you!—brought to light by your self-marketing efforts.

  - To simply create a new job for you to do work that was needed but undefined. For example, a large trade association may need a better business development program. Your resume as an experienced and highly productive "major accounts" sales representative for a major hotel chain might lead to the creation of a similar job within that large trade association to sell sponsorships and affiliate memberships to that industry's vendors.

So dig out your address book, your list of contacts in your e-mail address book, and your stack of collected business cards, and start making those calls! Remember, you are working from a script, so get that in writing before you begin.

Summary

- The hidden and unpublished job market is a great source of jobs—don't overlook it.

- To tap it requires a well-planned self-marketing approach and a good network.

- Utilize your network fully, and continue to build it—forever!

- Make the calls, and follow your scripts.

CHAPTER 10

Moving from the Government (Including the Military) to the Private Sector

Leaving the government (including the military) to find a job in the private sector presents some unique twists to the job-seeking process ... and a little culture shock.

This is a two-step process:

1. Your first task is to learn and understand how the private sector works and what it expects from those that work there.

2. Your second task is to learn what is different compared to your government working environment.

In both cases, it will probably call for some purposeful adaptation on your part.

1. What are the expectations of employers in the private sector?

   • It is very simple. Get the work done—on time and error-free— with the fewest people possible at the lowest cost possible and with no problems. See the reference to the "high output, low cost, no problems" discussion in chapter 1.

   • The expectation is that people will show up on time and work a full workday with the mission of helping their departments and therefore the entire organization prosper and achieve its goals.

   • The expectation is that people will understand how their jobs fit into the whole scheme of things and how their contributions impact the whole organization.

- The expectation is that people will think proactively about how to do their work; innovation and "thinking out of the box" is desired in the private sector.

- The expectation of private sector employers is for everyone to have a "customer service" attitude—even those that do not interact with the organization's "customers." The "customers" of those workers are those that they serve internally.

- The expectation of the private sector is that teamwork and team play are the norm.

2. What is very different about working in the private sector compared to working in government?

   - You can "break the rules"—take reasonable risks and even make mistakes—and survive. Often, innovation comes about as a result of this risk taking.

   - There is less hierarchy in the private sector and much more of a collegial approach between supervisors and subordinates. At the same time, the boss is still the boss.

   - There is less structure in the private sector when it comes to getting the work done. People are cross-trained to lend a hand or even take over a function as necessary. The "that isn't my department" approach is not tolerated in the private sector.

   - There is no "spend it or lose it" mind-set in the budgeting process; it's just the opposite. Not spending all that was budgeted, whether for goods and services or staff headcount, is good in the private sector.

   - The private sector usually pays better (not always; it depends on the position) but at the expense of benefits. There are virtually no defined benefit retirement plans in the private sector. Private sector retirement plans are usually based upon a 401(k) plan, which is a defined contribution plan where you can contribute a portion of your income pretax into a variety of investment funds that you direct. Since you self-direct these contributions, it requires you to be somewhat of a knowledgeable investor or to key in on the advice your 401(k) administrator provides. Health care benefits are usually more expensive and last only while employed versus those of military retirees, for example, that continue past the time of retirement.

- There is less "job security" in the private sector. Your job continuing as an entry on the organizational chart—and your occupation of it—is highly dependent on a variety of factors discussed in chapter 1 and elsewhere in this book versus the relatively secure tenure of many or most government jobs.

- The private sector provides far fewer days off for holidays and usually fewer also for sick leave and vacation.

- The private sector, by and large, operates in a Microsoft world—relatively current operating system and business-oriented software. Some organizations use Apple's Mac software, but it is not as prevalent as Microsoft. Oftentimes the government has developed its own software or runs on older versions of standard business software. Therefore, you may well need to get up to speed on computer software programs and operating systems.

3.   If you are leaving the military, here are some additional thoughts as your prepare to enter the private sector:

- Be very judicious with your "war stories" and how you compare work in the private sector with your previous military employment. Those who you work with will be grateful for your service to the country but generally do not want to hear about it every day.

- Watch the alphabet soup means of communicating. Use real words, the same words your coworkers use. No "G-2" for "information." You are no longer going to be "deployed" anywhere; you will be assigned or sent to locations.

- If you were an officer, recognize that in your military life, people obeyed ... or else. Ahhhh ... not in the civilian world because you can't lock them up for disobeying <smile>. So "disobey" sometimes they do. Approach giving orders as "giving directives"—approaching people you wish to do something in a collaborative manner—and explaining, if it isn't obvious, how it all fits together.

- Watch your demeanor, especially if you were a higher-level officer. You will usually find in the civilian world that the leaders there—CEOs and the like—work very hard to not let their lofty ranks become apparent in their demeanors. While they have the trappings of authority, they don't walk and talk in a manner to flaunt it. A warm smile is the way of the civilian world (even when things go wrong), not a cold icy stare. Remember that, and it will make your transition much smoother and more productive.

- You need to develop an "elevator talk speech" for your new role. We all have one – yours now is descriptive of your military work. An elevator talk speech is a definitive and short presentation of what you do and who you do it for. An example would be: "I recently retired from the Army after twelve years of service and now am a HR manager at XYZ firm. I am primarily involved in benefits administration for our U.S. operatons.

- Learn to dress for your "new world." In many cases, you either wore a uniform (no fashion choices) or wore very, very casual clothes. Ever visit a US Postal Service regional mail-sorting center? Very, very casual dress prevails. Read a fashion magazine—both women and men! No plastic pocket protectors and industrial strength watchbands or shoes. Observe the dress of your civilian friends who have jobs like that to which you aspire. And watch those PX aviator glasses. The frames are not only a dead giveaway but also geeky. Sorry about that, General! Just as the military has a several-day "general officer charm school" for first-time general officers, you need the same kind of orientation to enter the civilian world of work. It just needs to be self-taught!

- Note that there are staffing service firms that specialize in placing certain classifications of military personnel. Most commonly, they assist service academy graduates when they leave after their first tour of duty as well as non-commissioned officers retiring from the military. Do a Google search for "military staffing" and "military staffing agencies".

Summary

- Be aware of the expectations of the private sector:

  - Get the work done—on time, error-free, for the least amount of money.

  - Give full time and energy in a collaborative manner.

  - Understand how the job fits in to the whole organizational effort.

  - Have a 100% customer service attitude at all times.

- Know what is different in the private sector:

  - You can take risks and still be a winner.

  - There is less hierarchy.

  - There is less structure—people daily cross work zones to get the work done.

  - There is no "spend it or lose it" regarding budgets.

  - Private sector pays more but at the expense of benefits.

  - There is less job security.

- For military folks making the transition, remember the following:

  - Curtail the war stories.

  - Talk real words; no alphabet soup words.

  - Know how to get things done without "ordering" it.

  - Develop a elevator talk speech.

  - Dress for your new world of work.

  - Take advantage of staffing services that focus on the military.

CHAPTER 11

Congratulations! You Have an Offer! Now What?
Evaluating Job Offers; Negotiating Salary and Benefits

Hurrah! Finally, an offer! This is what you have been working toward. Good for you. Now is it the right offer for you?

Evaluating offers

In times of low unemployment, offers come quickly and frequently; employers are desperate to fill the job. Every day the job sits empty, either work is not getting done or others are on overload to pick up those tasks and responsibilities. Simply put, it is somewhat of a job-seekers market.

Conversely, when there are many people looking for work, employers can be far more selective.

The important thing from your perspective is that you accept the offer that is "right" for you.

Ideally, as the hiring process has progressed, you have learned more and more about the employer, its mission, and its people and culture. By now, you should know what your prospective boss is like and whether or not the two of you "clicked." You should have a very good understanding of what will be expected of you. These are the criteria you need to know in order to evaluate whether the job is indeed right for you.

At the same time, wouldn't it be nice to have something to compare the offer to, such as another offer?

Now think back to Thanksgiving dinner. The cook's challenge is to have the potatoes done at the same time as the turkey, the green beans, and the corn (at least that is what the menu is for Thanksgiving dinner at my home!). The point is timing. The same concept applies to seeking your next job. Wouldn't it be nice if all the offers you were going to get came within a day of each other—especially if you were unemployed and hence far less picky than if you already had a job? Of course it would. So your job is to see if you can stall some forthcoming offers (without losing them, of course) and hasten some others so that the offers you do get of interest all occur at about the same time. If working with a staffing firm, their mission is the same—for you to have a choice of job offers that all come through within a few days of each other.

You can stall on an offer no more than a day—two at the most. I remember clearly a candidate that had not made a decision two days after getting a great offer. When I asked him for a status report, he told me that he and his wife were still talking about it. I said, "What else can you possibly be talking about after two days? All of the details of the offer have been coming together over the past ten days you have been interviewing with XYZ. Either you want it or you don't. My client, your prospective employer, is going to rescind their offer if you don't act on it. Sorry about that, but look at their side of things. They need to get someone in that job pronto, and you don't want them thinking you aren't excited about the prospect of working for them. What is it about the job that causes your hesitation?" Our discussion revealed that there was no material issue preventing him from taking the offer other than the normal human reluctance to make a significant decision. We reviewed all the reasons he wanted to change jobs in the first place—his goals and career objectives—and he accepted the offer. As far as I know, he is still there!

Yes, it is nice to be able to compare offers to make a decision. However, don't get hung up on that if the offer you do have meets your minimum criteria. Clearly, your current employment status comes into play. If you are currently employed, you can be far more selective about accepting and turning down offers. Just don't lose a job you would really like while waiting to generate another offer so you can compare.

If you are unemployed, unless you have a fat bank account, you *never* turn down a job offer that meets your minimum requirements without another bona fide job offer.

At the same time, you don't want to accept an offer out of desperation, only to leave it a few weeks later when a better situation comes along. The solution is to continually qualify and continually evaluate all of the aspects of a job as they develop over the course of interviews and your research. Ask the questions needed to really know what life will be like in each job after six months on the job. Once it becomes apparent that it isn't for you, tell all involved that you are no longer interested, and gracefully back away.

But wait. What if you are unemployed? It depends on what your prospects are for other offers and the size of the nest egg you are living on. It also depends if you are also working as a temporary employee with an income that pays at least the basic bills. As noted above, if you are unemployed, you *never* turn down a job offer without serious thought.

So what do you do if the one and only job offer you have, with nothing else on the horizon, is a job you really don't want? You have a decision to make. Take the following into consideration:

- You need to look out for yourself, so if that means taking a job you don't want out of desperation, just recognize that you must perform or you will unemployed again soon.

- If you accept the job and then leave within a short period of time, you have done a disservice to the employer (and staffing firm if you worked through them). This in turn will not endear you to either of them regarding references, and the staffing firm will probably no longer work on your behalf.

With all that said, let's review how to evaluate an offer. Well before you get an offer, you have thought through carefully what your objectives are, what your strengths and soft areas are, and what you like to do and don't like to do. You have considered such factors as travel and hours, as they impact "quality of life" issues. You know where the career track of a job is likely to take you, and you know if you wish to pursue it (the next job is probably relocation to the home office in Dallas, and that is okay) or not pursue it (there is no way you want to relocate to the home office in Dallas). In other words, you have thought through all your parameters, and you have a feel for whether or not it meets a sufficient number of your criteria to accept it or not.

If working with a staffing service, they will take you through the decision-making process from the very beginning for each job you interview for—"If they offer you $XX, and if the job is A and B as well as C, are your prepared to accept it?"

The evaluation process for a single offer should be pretty simple: either it meets enough of your criteria or it doesn't.

What if you have more than one offer?

Work through each one individually as noted above, and see how they compare. These are the main criteria for comparison:

Criteria 1	Perceived opportunity for growth within the position and organization
Criteria 2	Perceived relationship with boss and if he/she will be a good boss; will you learn and grow in this job?
Criteria 3	General conditions and trends for the organization and its industry
Criteria 4	Reputation of the organization and its industry
Criteria 5	Salary and benefits
Criteria 6	Location, commute, access to public transportation
Criteria 7	General working conditions; working environment
Criteria 8	Overall quality of life issues—travel, hours, overtime
Criteria 9	"Other"—gut feeling about the job, the organization, the people you have met

It may be helpful to develop a matrix to help evaluate. Rate each criterion for each firm on a scale of 1 to 5, with 1 being unacceptable and 5 being perfect:

Criteria	Job "A"	Job "B"	Job "C"
Criteria 1	3	4	4
Criteria 2	3	3	3
Criteria 3	4	5	3
Criteria 4	3	3	3
Criteria 5	5	5	4
Criteria 6	2	4	4
Criteria 7	4	4	5
Criteria 8	4	4	3
Criteria 9	5	4	4
Totals	33	36	33

There are two things to note:

First, if you have been doing your qualifying and evaluating along the way, there should never be any rating lower than a 3 for the really important criteria. You may choose to accept a crummy location, poor quality of life due to much travel, or a shaky reputation of the industry or organization, but never accept a boss who you feel will not be a good boss and from whom you will learn. Never accept a job with no growth opportunity. If you really don't know how to rate one of the criteria for a particular offer, rate it average, a 3.

Secondly, don't be surprised if your matrix looks this close. If there were wide differences, it would mean that you didn't do a good job of the qualifying and evaluating along the way.

If you can make a decision as a result of this exercise, great. Recognize that you don't know now what you will know for sure after six months on the job, so put a fair amount of weight on criteria number nine—your gut feelings about the whole package of what you know about each job.

Don't hesitate to talk through this decision with those whose opinions your trust and who know you. It is an important decision.

Negotiating salary and benefits

The time to negotiate salary and benefits is after you have received a job offer. Why not earlier? Because you don't want to negotiate against yourself. Your employer contact knows your compensation history and knows the compensation range for the job he or she is trying to fill (and hopefully you know the range also!). This person is aware of all the answers you and other candidates have given during the interviewing process. Your employer contact has also made comparisons of whom else they have been interviewing for the job and how large the pool is of people to choose from (your competition for the job). From this base of information, a decision will be made as to whom to make the offer and at what salary. These factors will determine if the offer is at the high end of the range or not. Another factor that enters into the formula is your current employment status; if you were employed, the offer may be higher than if you were unemployed. The benefit package is probably formula driven for the position you are interviewing for, so there is little opportunity to tinker with it.

What then do you negotiate? Actually, very little. If the salary range is $45,000–$50,000, and your last salary was $46,500, and the offer comes in at $47,000 or $47,500, yes, you are disappointed it wasn't more. Recognize, however, that it is an increase, and be assured that the hiring official thought it through and felt that the offer was a fair one. In almost every case, the salary detailed in the job offer has been carefully thought through, the employer wanting to pay as low an amount as is reasonable to attract and hire the talent to do the job. If you ask for an adjustment because you don't feel it is enough, you are not sending the best of messages!

The best approach is to prenegotiate the salary during the interview process. Recall the discussion noted in the interviewing chapter.

Considering the following if the interviewer asks, "What salary are you looking for?":

- Answer carefully. Hopefully you know the salary range ahead of time. If so, you answer, "Well, I know the salary range is $X to $Y. My last salary and bonus plan paid $Z on an annual basis. While I would like to be at the high end of your range, I am primarily looking for opportunity first and am prepared to be flexible about the compensation package."

- If you don't know the range, then you answer, "Well, my last salary and bonus plan paid $Z on an annual basis. While I would prefer to make some upward strides, I am primarily looking for opportunity first and am prepared to be flexible about the compensation package." Never inflate your current or past compensation. It is not uncommon for an employer to ask to see a W-2, and you are sunk if it doesn't match what you have said.

- By these responses, you have put a salary number on the table.

If for some reason you aren't asked this question, toward the end of the interview, say, "We haven't discussed compensation. What is the range?" And from there, offer the first response above.

What can sometimes be negotiated are some minor aspects in the area of benefits—getting on the employer's health plan sooner than the normal waiting period, clearing during the interview that you have made travel reservations for a family reunion at a distant location and therefore need more vacation leave time than might normally be available, perhaps getting paid parking, and so on. Be aware, however, that your employer likes standardization of benefits within a class or group of employees; it avoids the hard feelings that arise when workers doing the same or similar jobs find out there is a difference in their benefits plans.

Keep in mind that one of the advantages of working with a staffing service is that they can negotiate on your behalf without you personally interacting with the prospective employer.

Do keep in mind that what you are looking for is opportunity to learn and grow, to work for a boss who will be a mentor, and to be part of a team. Don't get hung up on a salary if it is within your realistic range—and remember that the money will take care of itself if you do a knockout job.

Summary

- Evaluate and qualify every potential offer during the entire interview and selection process.

- While it is nice to have offers to choose from, don't lose a good one waiting for others to materialize.

- Build a matrix to help make a decision between two or more offers.

- Don't overlook your "gut" feeling about a particular job offer.

- If unemployed, *never* turn down an offer without really serious thought.

- There is usually not much to negotiate regarding salary and benefits when you get an offer; trying to wring out every last dollar is a big mistake.

CHAPTER 12

Parting Is Such Sweet Sorrow—Resigning

Just as there has been a right way and a wrong way for the steps you took to find your new job, so shall there be to resigning.

Unless your supervisor is aware of your plans to resign, recognize that your resignation will cause disruption and problems and perhaps major issues for your supervisor to cope with. Therefore, be sensitive to the timing of your resignation and how you do it. I recall the resignation of a sales representative I will call Sally, who resigned by calling me on my cell when I was some 150 miles away, zipping along at sixty-five miles per hour on my way to a week of vacation—yikes! Don't pull a "Sally" on your boss—it just isn't fair!

Monday is the best day of the week to resign

Mondays are always better than any other day of the week, as it gives several business days to get the word out to others and begin the process of taking care of the workload pending a new hire or reassignment of duties. A Friday resignation often means an imbalance of information since some people will know and discuss over the weekend and others won't (there are *no* secrets when it comes to resignations!).

When it comes time to resign, do so in a positive and matter-of-fact manner, particularly if you and your supervisor don't have the best of relationships. There is no need to rehash past issues. Simply say something like, "Bill, I need to give you my two weeks' notice. I need to move on. It has been great working here, and I will do what I can to help with the transition."

Never, never, never use your resignation as a platform to make a statement or speech or to give someone a "piece of your mind." The

136

operative phrase is "burn no bridges." You never know what the future may hold! Remember, your boss is the one a prospective employer may look to for a reference someday. Act accordingly!

Notice

Normally two weeks' notice is sufficient, but if your new employer has set a start date further out than two weeks, you can offer more notice if you wish. At the same time, recognize that your current employer might not want you hanging around, depending on the circumstances, in which case, you may be asked to wrap things up in a day or two and then depart.

Be prepared for a buyback—a counteroffer

If you have been doing a great job and getting along with your supervisor, all of a sudden, you have thrown a monkey wrench into the organizational chart. This is especially true if it is a busy time of the year or you have been working on a new project and so on. It is not uncommon for your boss to ask "What would it take to keep you here?" or "How much is your new salary going to be? I'll match it." Do keep in mind why you looked for and found a new position. The offer for more money, a different assignment, and the like were forthcoming because you gave notice. It is not as a result of appreciation for you and your work. There is no assurance you will be any better taken care of in the future once you rescind your resignation and stay with your current employer. Furthermore, you may well be viewed as "damaged goods"; after all, you were prepared to "fire" your employer. With rare exceptions, you should not accept a buyback.

Should I tell my boss I want to look for a new job?

A question I am often asked is this: "Once I have made up my mind to search for a new job, should I share that with my supervisor?" Probably not. Your boss's loyalty is to his boss and the organization he or she works for. Your boss will probably do what is right for the organization and make plans for your imminent departure, the timing of which may not sync with you interviewing and then getting an offer. You don't want to do what would seem to be the fair thing and then find yourself unemployed because your replacement was hired before you found your new job! There may be rare exceptions, but best keep your plans to change jobs to yourself until it is time to give notice.

Summary

- Resign gracefully.

- Resign on a Monday.

- Give two weeks' notice.

- Be prepared for a buyback—a counteroffer. It is usually not a good idea to accept it.

- Keep your job search confidential, no matter how much you want to "do the right thing" and tell your supervisor.

CHAPTER 13

Showtime—Day One at Your New Job!

Objective accomplished, right? Well, almost!

Yes, you have a new job, but you aren't yet done with the process.

In fact, the process will take upward of six months to a year for most positions. Your new objective is to be this:

- Highly productive

- Low cost

- Not a "problem"

Sound familiar? From chapter 1, it is what your new employer and new boss want from you. And if you were hired to be the boss, it is what your board of directors wants from you. As you begin your new job, keep these three objectives firmly in mind. It is how, overall, you will be judged.

Your first days on the job

Approach day one just as you did your interview: carefully. Same for day two, three, and four!

Have the same smile for everyone, same confident walk and handshake, and same attention to your appearance.

You want everyone you come into contact with to go home and tell a spouse or significant other, "We have a new person on board, and he (or she) seems to be one of the nicest people I have ever met." That is the impact you want to make!

Show respect for the "territory" of others. When you are assigned to an office or a workstation, take personalizing it slowly. See what others have done. I had a new employee who within days festooned his work area with photos that were too goth for even the broad-minded—which had me thinking, "What was he thinking?"

Recognize that "you don't know what you don't know"

There are four levels of competence:

1. Unconscious incompetence—you don't know what you don't know; you don't know how to do something, but you don't know that until the time comes to try it

2. Conscious incompetence—you know what you don't know; you don't know how to do something, and you are aware of that fact

3. Conscious competence—you know what you know; you know how to do something, but you need to focus and concentrate on how to do it

4. Unconscious competence—you know what you know so well that you do it without thinking

Mark Twain said it well with his great quote, "It ain't what you don't know that gets you into trouble. It's what you know for sure that just ain't so!"

Keep these in mind as you begin your new job. You don't want to "out-run your blockers," moving ahead without really knowing what you are doing but thinking that you do!

Take notes, ask questions, read whatever handbook you are given, and observe what others do and how they do it.

Be very slow to tell someone, "Here's how we did it at my last job." Trust me—no one wants to hear that comment. After a period of time, you can say, "From my experience, I can see that there might be a different approach."

Ask for or identify a helpful peer

Depending on the position for which you are hired, some employers will give you an assigned resource—someone other than your supervisor to help answer questions and give nonsupervisory guidance.

If that doesn't happen, ask your supervisor, "Who is the 'go to' person in the department?" This may well be the person who can help you considerably in the transition into the new job.

Good luck!

Summary

- Remember, your job is to be productive, low cost, and no problems.

- Go slowly the first week or two until you get the hang of it all.

- Recognize you don't know all you need to know.

- Have someone help you learn the ropes.

CHAPTER 14

Now What—Planning Your Career

Some time has gone by, and you have settled well into your new job. New routines, new challenges, and new opportunities present themselves to you. Wonderful!

However, chances are you are not going to spend the rest of your working career in the same job or even with the same employer.

You want *every* future job move to be done on your terms and under your control as much as possible. That means having a game plan, just as you did (hopefully with the help of this book) for your most recent job search.

The game plan for the future

1. Engage in networking, networking, and more networking.

2. Stay current in all you do and know; remember, job security resides in skill sets.

3. Make sure you are a "go to" person in your organization.

4. Cultivate staffing service contacts.

5. Manage your career.

Let's examine each of these in some detail.

1. Engage in networking, networking, and more networking

If you didn't buy or borrow at a library Harvey Mackay's book *Dig Your Well Before You're Thirsty*, do it now. The book is both a guide and a tutorial for networking, with countless examples of techniques for building a network.

Look for networking opportunities locally. I am an amateur Civil War historian. There exists throughout the country something called Civil War roundtables. They meet monthly for a presentation, oftentimes by an author, and they usually include a dinner or cocktail reception. I belong to three of them. I don't go to all the meetings, but I get their monthly newsletters and have a membership list for each of them. I have made contacts there that have been good for my business.

Similar opportunities no doubt exist for you based upon your interests. Cultivate them. Don't use the membership list for marketing purposes; that kind of activity will get you tossed out of the organization. Rather, use the membership list to target some people you want to get to know better by sitting next to them and engaging them in conversation. If the membership list doesn't include their places of employment, often their e-mail addresses will give it away; otherwise, do Google searches to identify contacts that might be of current or future value. Make a point of getting to know them at the organization's events and so on.

Find a creative way to stay in periodic contact with members of your network. I mentioned earlier sending holiday cards as one approach. Another approach is to send clippings of articles of general business interest to your business contacts, articles about tennis to your tennis contacts, book recommendations to your network contacts that you know are avid readers, and so on. You get the picture.

If you belong to a gym or health club, the time and place to establish contacts is usually in the locker room; most people working out want to focus on the task at hand and are often "plugged in" to their music. I have found that the locker room is a place to say "What's that book that you're reading?" or "I see you are a Big Ten alum—me too" or whatever. A good 10–15% of the books I have read over the years have come about from locker room referrals. In the process, I have made many a contact that has been good for my business—contacts that became consultants that I have used, contacts that have become clients, and contacts that became valued vendors to my company.

No doubt there are trade associations and/or professional societies for your industry. Pursue being appointed to a committee. You will be doing something of value *and* meeting and interfacing with new people—people you can add to your network.

Judiciously invite others to connect to you on LinkedIn. See what LinkedIn groups might be good ones for you to join.

Building a network is an active process and one you can pursue on almost a daily basis. The payoff will be there in proportion to how large and effective your network is.

2. Stay current in all you do and know; remember, job security resides in skill sets

It all starts with curiosity—curiosity about the pros and cons of the newest PC operating system; the newest version of Microsoft Office; and what will be the impact of the upcoming changes to legislation and regulation; about the best way to address a particular business issue or problem that leads you to research, read, and discuss.

Wisdom comes from knowledge, and knowledge comes from curiosity. It will be very difficult to keep your skill sets up to date if you don't read and absorb. A daily newspaper is a must, and if you are in the business world, add the *Wall Street Journal* to your list. If your local daily newspaper isn't very far reaching and comprehensive, add the *New York Times* to your daily reading.

Include a trade journal or two of your profession or area of employment.

When you read, ponder what you have read. It is one thing to know that ABC Company spun off its XYZ division. The question is, what was the CEO's rationale, and what are the expected results? If it made the news, the follow-up also will make the news. You aren't going to study the subject, but you do want to generally know the logic and rationale behind decisions made and how accurate were the predicted results. Then when someday you have to make a similar decision, you have a basis of understanding the path others have traveled before you. Every decision in a workplace environment you will ever make has been made before by someone else. Your objective is to know what decisions were made and what the short- and long-term outcomes were. The greater your mental inventory of these "case studies," the more you bring to the table in terms of decision-making ability.

When a workplace situation arises, you want to be able to contribute the history of similar decisions in the past. This is often referred to as "organizational history"; successful organizations have it, and it keeps mistakes form occurring. You want to be one of those that possess it.

3.   Make sure you are a "go to" person in your organization

As we have mentioned before, the "go to" people in an organization are the ones that others turn to for advice, decisions and input. Because of this degree of contribution to the organization, the "go to" people are valued employees beyond the performance of their job descriptions. This translates into job security. "Go to" people are normally not laid off when the time comes to cut staff.

4.   Cultivate staffing service contacts

From time to time, you may be asked for advice by friends and acquaintances regarding job changes and career moves. You want to be able to refer them to one or two trusted and highly competent staffing service recruiters. Why? There are two reasons:

a.   You are helping someone who in turn will be grateful and therefore be an enhanced member of your network. You can call upon him or her to return the favor one day as may be appropriate. You never know where your and his or her career paths will evolve and perhaps connect.

b.   The recruiters you refer him or her to will value you for sending talent their way and will keep *you* in mind for those opportunities that are a possibility for you.

As your recruiter's career proceeds, it will give you increasing exposure to those opportunities that might be of value to you.

Don't limit your contact to just a single recruiter. It is better to have two at two different staffing services. Multiply the value of these contacts.

At the same time, be sure you know—at least on a speaking basis—the recruiter's boss, the general manager of the staffing service. If and when your recruiter changes firms, you will not have lost the connection with the staffing firm if you have multiple contacts there.

5. Manage your career

Longevity in a job is great as long as you are learning and growing. Managing your career means thinking ahead to what you perceive at the time is your ultimate career objective and then creating a plan to achieve it. Your ultimate objective may well change as time goes on, but if it is—as of now—to be a senior lending officer in a major bank, think ahead of the steps to get there. It may mean leaving a good job for a great job.

What you don't want to happen is for your career to manage you, taking whatever comes your way. You want to manage the process.

Pay attention to the trends in your industry and profession. If you are a sales manager in print journalism (newspaper or magazine), the best time to move may have passed you by. Print journalism has been in a steady decline for several years, and the trend is projected to continue. When you see trends that don't bode well, it is time to strongly consider making a change!

Summary

- Obviously you don't want to be a job-hopper, changing jobs every twelve to eighteen months. By the same token, however, always be exploring and open to making a change if it makes good sense to do so.

- Keep the following in mind:

  1. Engage in networking, networking, and more networking.

  2. Stay current in all you do and know; remember, job security resides in skill sets.

  3. Make sure you are a "go to" person in your organization.

  4. Cultivate staffing service contacts.

  5. Manage your career.